The New SRI LANKAN House

The New SRI LANKAN House

Robert Powell

Photography by
Sebastian Posingis

Essays by
David Robson

TALISMAN

Contents

HOUSES ON THE EDGE

CITY HOUSES

New Directions in Tropical Architecture in Sri Lanka

Robert Powell

In February 2014, accompanied by David Robson and photographer Sebastian Posingis, I embarked on a journey to chart the development of private houses in Sri Lanka in the early 21st century. During the civil war, there was not a lot of money around for building, but several architects did produce good work in times of austerity. Since then, the ongoing peace process has seen a rise of confidence in the urban middle classes and a large number of private houses have resulted. These include urban residences in Colombo, villas in the suburbs, beachfront homes on the southern coast and rural retreats inland — many of which are showcased in this book.

Twenty-six houses represent the work of 21 architects most of whom are 'home grown'. All were born after independence in 1948. Ten obtained their first degree from the Department of Architecture at the University of Moratuwa (UOM), while five qualified via the part-time course at the City School of Architecture (CSA) within the Sri Lanka Institute of Architects in Colombo. Five of the architects pursued undergraduate or postgraduate studies in the UK, at University College London, University of North London, University of East London or the University of Brighton and one studied in Finland.

Nineteen of the houses are designed by the 'next generation' of Sri Lankan architects all of whom commenced in practice after 1998, the year that Geoffrey Bawa's practice effectively closed. The architects include Godridge Samuel (52), Vinod Jayasinghe (51), Amila De Mel (50), Channa Daswatte (49), Thisara Thanapathy (49), Ranjan Aluwihare (48), Ragi Kadirgamar (47), Kumudu Munasinghe (45), Pradeep Kodikara (45), Palinda Kannangara (44), Philip Weeraratne (44), Sanath Liyanage (43), Shayan Kumaradas (42), Waruna Gomis (37) and Sudesh Nanayakkara (36).

There are four houses by architects who span the Bawa-era and the 'next generation'. C Anjalendran (63), Vijitha Basnayaka (60) and Madhura Prematilleke (57) have been influential teachers in the two architectural schools in Sri Lanka in addition to being practicing architects. Most of the younger generation has encountered them (and in some cases been profoundly influenced by them) in their formative years. While Anjalendran 'carries the torch' for Bawa as illustrated in the Malalasekara House and the Ranatunga House, Prematilleke and Basnayaka have a markedly different approach to design as illustrated in the Green House at Digana and the Kishan Perera House in Pelawatte.

The remaining three houses are designed by two internationally respected Japanese architects, 57-year-old Shigeru Ban and Tadao Ando (72), both winners of the prestigious Pritzker Prize for Architecture, and the renowned Australian architect Kerry Hill (71), winner of an Aga Khan Award for Architecture and the Gold Medal of the Royal Australian Institute of Architects.

A House in the Tropics

During a meeting with Geoffrey Bawa in 1995, we talked at length about design in the tropics and he suggested a number of criteria by which to assess a successful dwelling design. "Life in Ceylon (he used the former name)," he said, "is about living out-of-doors." He was referring to the in-between spaces in the form of terraces, shaded verandahs and balconies that typify the best houses in the tropics. He also asserted that, "a house in the tropics is about living in close proximity to the natural world and one should not destroy any substantial trees on the site." Then Bawa added another criteria that is more problematic. "A house in the tropics," he said, "should be designed with the minimal use of glass."

The Cinnamon Hill House (above), designed by Bawa and completed in 1993, exemplifies this approach. Revolving around a tall open-sided living space facing southeast, Bawa manipulated the plan, arranging walls and columns so that existing trees were retained — one even grows in the bathroom! Glass is almost entirely eliminated and replaced by shutters and timber louvres, so that the interior is naturally ventilated. It is perhaps the simplest house I have ever encountered, certainly it made a huge and lasting impression upon me and established a benchmark by which I would thereafter judge every house in the tropics.

Over the course of the next decade, I gleaned other criteria. From the Indian architect Charles Correa I learned to appreciate the open-to-sky courtyard and what Correa refers to as "the blessings of the sky". Many of Correa's most potent architectural ideas were developed through the design of individual houses where "open-to-sky space is of crucial importance for it can make the difference between livable habitat and claustrophobia."[1] Correa emphasised "the complex manifestations of built form in a warm climate where between closed-box and open-to-sky there lies a continuum of zones with varying definitions and degrees of protection …. The boundaries between these various zones are not formal and sharply demarcated, but easy and amorphous. Subtle modulations of light, of the quality of ambient air, register each transition in our senses."[2]

Later, the Malaysian architect Jimmy C Y Lim reminded me of his simple strategy for designing houses in monsoon Asia. "We have an excess of sun, so I keep the sun out. We have lots of rain, so I attempt to keep

Page 1: Villa Vista designed by Shigeru Ban.
Page 2: The Green House at Eagles Ridge, Digana designed by Madhura Prematilleke overlooks the Victoria Dam.
Pages 6–7: High mountains and verdant rice fields create an idyllic setting for the Kalundewa Retreat at Dambulla designed by Sanath Liyanage.
Previous page: The two-storey Channa Daswatte House in Madiwela is only one room wide, therey encouraging the through passage of air.
Opposite top: The temperature in the Malalasekera House by C Anjalendran is reduced by the non-reflective surfaces of the garden.
Opposite bottom: The Kishan Perera house by Vijitha Basnayaka is planned around a tall open-to-sky atrium.
Above left and right: In the Cinnamon Hill House (1993) Geoffrey Bawa eschewed the use of glass.

Right: The Kalundewa Retreat by Sanath Liyanage is shaded by trees and cooled by a man-made lake.
Below: Sensible orientation and overhanging eaves cool the Siva and Vasuki House designed by Shayan Kumaradas.
Bottom: The surrounding trees and a timber pergola provide shade for the verandah in the Guava House by Ranjan Aluwihare.

the rain out. We need a lot of shade, so I provide it by having lots of trees. We consequently have lots of leaves so we should not have gutters as blocked gutters are useless. Because we are living in a hot, humid climate we should have cross-ventilation".[3]

The spirit of a house in the tropics is formed by merging the dwelling with its surroundings, thereby creating ambiguous and intermediary spaces. The garden thus provides non-reflective surfaces and serves the functional purpose of modifying the climate, reducing radiant heat and providing shade.

Geoffrey Bawa's initial criteria are thus expanded and a checklist for a house in the tropics would include:

- have a living/dining area which is the focus of the house and which is permanently open to external environment
- not destroy any substantial trees on the site and be in harmony with nature
- be designed with minimal glazing
- not have gutters
- be surrounded by a garden with non-reflective surfaces
- have wide overhanging eaves to provide shade
- have in-between spaces in the form of courtyards, verandahs, terraces and balconies
- have tall rooms to encourage convection cooling
- be naturally ventilated with permeable walls facing prevailing breezes
- be one-room deep with openings on opposite sides capable of being adjusted to create the *Venturi* effect.

The list is not entirely original or unprecedented, for as early as 1964 books such as *Tropical Architecture in the Dry and Humid Zones* by Maxwell Fry and Jane Drew[4] substantiated with technical data the validity of this model, much of it learned from the vernacular.

For residents of houses in Colombo there are other considerations. There is first the problem of dust, pollution and noise. It is arguably a necessity to combat these conditions with air-conditioners, at least in bedrooms. There are also problems of security that can be addressed by enclosing the site in a high wall. Another approach is to incorporate duality into the plan arrangement where the street façade has the appearance of an exclusive enclosure while the façade facing the garden is comparatively open.

During a seminar I attended in Zanzibar in 1987, Hasan-Uddin Khan and Charles Moore introduced the notion of a house as a 'Fortress of Solitude' and argued that what makes the concept of home of the different typologies is that of retreat or solitude.[5] The notion of the house as a place for solitude is a recurring theme in the design of the houses in this book (see Pringiers House, pages 108–115 and Siva and Vasuki House, pages 70–77). Man seems to have a need for a place to be calm, quiet and to recreate oneself in a rapidly changing world. The checklist of criteria for a house in the tropics should therefore also include:

- in response to security issues, duality in the planning arrangements to give openness and direct access to a garden or court on one side with a closed and exclusive appearance on the public façade
- air-conditioning in selected areas of the house to overcome heat, humidity, noise, dust and pollution
- the use of shading and careful orientation to minimize the air-conditioning load
- the notion of 'retreat' or refuge
- increasing use of solar collectors and wind generators as their capital cost falls
- pools and fountains that contribute to cooling in addition to giving sensory pleasure.

The latter point reminds me of an intervention by Geoffrey Bawa during the seminar in Zanzibar. "Even if one uses the simplest of materials," he said, "if these are arranged satisfactorily, and if a certain amount of thought is given to landscape it can give a sense of belonging and pleasure. Pleasure cannot be omitted .... It is as important as shelter from the rain."[6]

In selecting the houses for inclusion in this book the above criteria were constantly referred to and guided the choice. There is no attempt to prioritise the criteria but the houses that are featured fulfill most, if not all, of the requirements of an exemplary house in the tropics. Some are admittedly deficient in one area while excelling in others. Two important issues are the use of glass vis-à-vis air-conditioning and the importance of orientation.

In many contemporary tropical houses glass is the ubiquitous material for any external opening. Glass keeps out the rain and by-and-large excludes flies, moths, mosquitoes, geckos, snakes, squirrels and monkeys. But the consequence is that it inevitably leads to the installation of air-conditioning. Air-conditioning solves many problems — it cools, it dehumidifies, it keeps out the insects — but it is hugely expensive both in terms of installation cost and in terms of energy usage and it cuts off the occupant of a house from the outside world. Many of the architects featured in this book are trying to resolve this dilemma.

If glass is to be used extensively, especially in east- and west-facing elevations it must be shaded. There are several ways this can be done: for example, by retaining existing trees and/or planting swiftly growing trees that cut out the sun in the morning and the late afternoon. This approach is well illustrated in the Green House designed by Madhura Prematilleke (see pages 62–69). Or the glass walls can be shaded by the use of louvres or tats (split bamboo and fabric screens) on the outside of the glass. There are a number of exemplary houses in this book illustrating this solution including the Maddumage House designed by Thisara Thanapathy (see pages 86–91) and the Channa Daswatte House (see pages 132–139). It is important to note that Venetian blinds or tats on the inside of the glass wall are useless in preventing heat gain — solar heat has already penetrated into the house and blinds on the inside do nothing to prevent this.

Houses should be orientated to face the prevailing wind. In most cases in Sri Lanka this will be the south west and the north east. But it is important to exclude torrential rain, which comes with the southwest monsoon. This can be achieved, to some extent, by

Top: Openable shutters and minimal glass promote cross-ventilation in the Channa Daswatte House.
Above: The section of the Maddumage House by Thisara Thanapathy is designed to shade glass used on the ground floor.

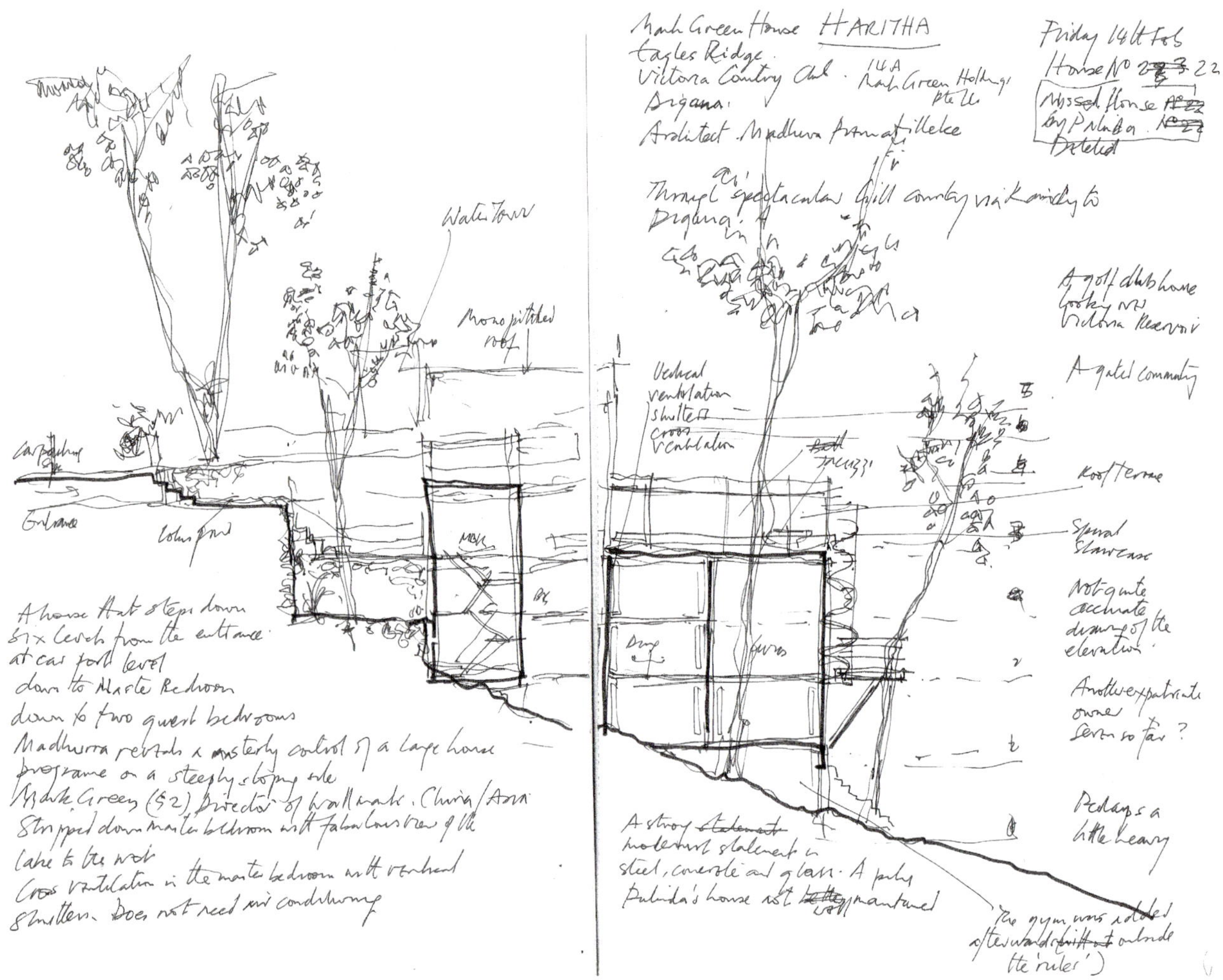

wide extended eaves and by deep verandahs. This will not prevent entirely the ingress of rain, which can be almost horizontal at the onset of a thunderstorm, but it does help to mitigate the effect.

Geoffrey Bawa's answer was to "use over-hanging roofs, but his interiors could be dark"[7] and there were critics of this approach. In 1997 Madhura Prematilleke criticised the so-called 'umbrella aesthetic' that, he said, "carries with it an idealization of rural, usually feudal life. It is an ideology that generates architectural models with an inherent anti-urban bias."[8]

Sustainable Dwellings

Since 1998 there has been an ongoing debate about how to create an architecture which is contemporary (ie how to escape from the vernacular umbrella), but which is also environmentally efficient and ecologically responsible.[9] It is anticipated that the houses within these pages will contribute to the debate.

Arguably, the greatest challenge for architects in the 21st century is to design houses that are sustainable, reduce the need for fossil fuels, have a low carbon footprint and respect the existing ecology. The architects whose work is illustrated here are alert to this and in a variety of ways are addressing the issues.

C Anjalendran has developed a highly appropriate robust aesthetic illustrated in the Ranatunga House at Nawala and the Malalasekara House at Borella (see pages 206–213 and pages 164–171 respectively). His houses are remarkably low energy. They give more for less. Anjalendran has said that every tree retained on the site is equivalent to one air-conditioner. The Green House at Digana by Madhura Premitilleke works well on a number of levels and includes cross ventilation and shading by the retention of mature trees. The slender plan is one-room-wide so that the dwelling has the benefit of natural ventilation and there are cleverly designed vertical pivoted opening vents alongside each of the large windows for this purpose. By opening these vents air movement can be induced by the *Venturi* effect without opening the sliding doors.

Vijitha Basnayaka promotes building with recycled materials, using corrugated metal sheets as interior wall cladding, bamboo 'tats', exposed steel structural columns and second-hand bricks in some of his houses. Amila de Mel's 2B1 House at Mirihana (see pages158–163) is a brilliantly inventive solution to the design of a tropical house: she utilises timber windows recycled from a demolished factory; doors were brought from her grandfather's house; and other recycled timber was utilized for floors. In Channa Daswatte's house at Madiwela the plan form is only one room wide so that there is excellent natural ventilation and in the Garden House in Colombo 7 the openness of the design both in the horizontal plane and the vertical plane ensures that there is an acute sense of living outdoors (see pages 178–185). The permeability also permits natural ventilation that is assisted by ceiling fans.

Thisara Thanapathy's design for the Maddumage House at Madawela is exemplary. Constructed largely with salvaged materials (timber and steel were transported to the site from a demolished factory in Colombo and the walkway is made of recycled railway sleepers), it proves that a building can be enchanting and environmentally responsible. The house works brilliantly, as does his award-winning design for the Abeyrathne House at Narahenpita, Colombo 5.

The Madanayake Retreat on pages 78–85 designed by Ragi Kadirgamar is completely self sufficient: rain-water is stored in large tanks for the dry months, and filtered using sand and carbon filters; solar panels supply hot water; much of the stone was salvaged from the old plantation house on the site; and the timber columns are five-year-old teak trees, felled and treated on the property. Other materials were sourced locally to

Opposite, top and above: The author's notebook recording the visit to each house in early 2015. **Opposite bottom:** Trees protect the glass wall of the Green House by Madhura Prematilleke. **Below:** The layered façade reduces solar heat gain in the Saffrons Beach House designed by Philip Weeraratne.

Above: The Kadju House by Pradeep Kodikara is orientated to catch the prevailing winds.
Below left: A deep light well in the centre of the plan assists in cross ventilation in the Malalasekara House by C Anjalendran.
Below right: An open stair creates a thermal chimney in the Ranatunga House by C Anjalendran.

reduce the carbon footprint. Ranjan Aluwihare's family retreat, the Guava House (see pages 32–39), is roofed with *iluk*, a reed obtained from Anaradapura that through a process of transpiration keeps the house cool.

Philip Weeraratne's two projects develop a convincing modernist idiom that takes into account sun-shading and cross-ventilation. Saffrons Beach House on pages 116–125 uses glass to protect against the monsoon (which can be ferocious in Habaraduwa), but the architect uses it in a creative way and the Siriwardena House at Mirihena is very sophisticated (see pages 214–219). Weeraratne has learned from his firm's collaboration with Tadao Ando and Shigeru Ban and he has produced better Sri Lankan architecture as a result.

In Godridge Samuel's house in Colombo (see pages 186–191) designed for his own family the green features of the house are exemplary — a central vertical ventilation shaft or 'chimney' provides natural ventilation by the 'stack effect' and the house is remarkably cool. Solar panels on the roof ensure the electricity bill is zero. In the Siva and Vasuki House designed by Shayan Kumaradas there are a variety of terraces, inside/outside spaces and shaded cool places with cross ventilation. There is no air-conditioning but the house is perfectly cool in its absence. The owners of the Kalundewa Retreat designed by Sanath Liyanage have built upon its natural assets, growing much of the produce consumed by their guests in sustainably farmed agriculture using traditional Sri Lankan farming methods (see pages 40–47).

Thus, it can be seen that there is a strong ecological ethic in the work of the leading Sri Lankan architects intent upon enhancing biodiversity and simultaneously advancing modern architecture.

Three globally acclaimed architects are included in the book. There can be no doubting Kerry Hill's credentials for he has lived and designed in the tropics for over 30 years. He acquired his residence at Armitage Hill in 1993 (see pages 54–61), and has steadily changed its dynamics over a period of two decades. The houses designed by Tadao Ando and Shigeru Ban (pages 108–115 and 100–107) are far more controversial. Both are climatically questionable, perhaps indicating their designer's unfamiliarity with the southwest monsoon. Yet the powerful geometry of Pringiers House at Mirissa by Ando speaks of man's (temporary) power over nature in the way it is imposed on the land. It is an exquisite piece of modern residential architecture that brilliantly meets the needs of its artist client while Villa Vista, designed by Shigeru Ban, has an exhilarating series of spaces culminating in the breathtaking (if occasionally wet) view of the Weligama Bay from the living room.

Above left: Louvred shutters assist in controlling cross ventilation at Villa Vista by Shigeru Ban. **Above centre:** Pavilions are arranged around a wonderful courtyard at Armitage Hill by Kerry Hill. **Above right:** In the Pringiers House, Tadao Ando creates a calm retreat from a hectic world.

This short essay is based on my personal engagement with Sri Lanka and it would be remiss of me not to acknowledge the contribution of important figures who shaped and influenced what the current generation of architects are doing, and with whom I have had no direct contact. The key names are Ulrik Plesner, Valentine Gunasekara and Minnette de Silva who are all mentioned in David Robson's introductory essay. Plesner's work is of particular importance since he collaborated with Bawa and influenced the following generation, particularly Anura Ratnavibhushana and Madhura Prematilleke.[10] Valentine Gunasekara also had a strong impact on this generation[11] as did his partner Chris de Saram, particularly as a teacher in the Department of Architecture at the University of Moratuwa.[12]

Envoi

It is evident that there are in Sri Lanka a number of creative young architects who are producing architecture that is comparable with the best in the world. In this book their work is placed alongside the acknowledged international master-architects Tadao Ando, Shigeru Ban and Kerry Hill.

I have termed these architects the 'next generation' and, taking their cue from their immediate predecessors, notably C Anjalendran, Anura Ratnavibhushana, Madhura Prematilleke and Vijitha Basnayaka they are creative, inventive, daring and resourceful, in the process contributing to a Sri Lankan architecture appropriate for the 21st century.

Endnotes

1 Correa, Charles, in an essay entitled 'Transfers and Transformations' in the monograph *Charles Correa* by Hasan-Uddin Khan, Concept Media, Singapore, 1987.
2 Correa, Charles, *ibid.*
3 Lim, Jimmy CS, in conversation with the author, 1995.
4 Fry, Maxwell and Jane Drew, *Tropical Architecture in the Dry and Humid Zones*, Batsford, London, 1964.
5 Khan, Hasan-Uddin and Charles Moore, 'The Architecture of the Individual House', in *The Architecture of Housing* (Robert Powell Ed.), *Exploring Architecture in Islamic Cultures*, The Aga Khan Trust for Culture, Geneva, 1990. pp 165-183.
6 Bawa, Geoffrey, in *The Architecture of Housing*, *Exploring Architecture in Islamic Cultures*, The Aga Khan Trust for Culture, Geneva,1990, p191.
7 Robson, David, in conversation by email, 5th May 2014.
8 Prematilleke, Madhura, 'Beyond the Umbrella and other Stories', Annual Session of the Sri Lanka Institute of Architects, February 1997.
9 Robson, David, in conversation with the author, 10th May 2014.
10 Plesner, Ulrik, *In Situ – An Architectural Memoir from Sri Lanka*, Narayana Press, Gyling, 2012.
11 Pieris, Anoma, *Imagining Modernity: The Architecture of Valentine Gunasekra*, Pannipitiya, Stamford Lake (Pte) Ltd, Colombo, 2007.
12 Madhura Prematilleke, in correspondence with the author, 4th June 2014.

At Home in Sri Lanka

David Robson

Sri Lanka lies close to the tip of India and a few degrees north of the equator. The sun cuts a near vertical arc across its skies and its climate is affected by two monsoons. A central mountain massif divides the island between a relatively dry zone to the north and east and a humid zone to the south-west. Today it is home to some twenty million people.

During the first millennium BC, the island's indigenous Stone Age inhabitants were displaced by waves of more sophisticated Iron Age folk from India who settled on the northern and eastern plains, introducing metal-work, irrigation and agriculture. These newcomers, the ancestors of the modern Sinhalese, are thought to have lived in simple houses of mud and wattle with roofs of thatch, arranged in clusters amongst the trees above their rice fields.

The Sinhalese established a civilization which flourished for over 1,000 years with magnificent cities and temples and palaces of great sophistication. Ordinary people, however, continued to live in simple mud houses.

In the wake of invasions from neighbouring India, this great civilization was finally brought to its knees during the 12th century and the Sinhalese abandoned the cities and irrigated farmlands of the plains to seek refuge in the thick forests of the central highlands. Here they continued to build houses with solid mud walls and overhanging thatch roofs, often arranged around loosely defined open spaces.

During the 16th century Portuguese seafarers reached Sri Lanka and gradually established a colonial presence in coastal areas, only to be displaced in the mid 17th century by rivals from the Dutch East India Company. Though the Portuguese and Dutch failed to occupy more than the periphery of the island, they effectively controlled the lucrative Spice Trade and, with it, the entire economy. During this period the coastal areas became more and more cosmopolitan while the central highlands around the royal town of Kandy remained cut off from the world.

Galle, Sri Lanka's oldest continuously inhabited town, was always a cosmopolitan place. Founded by Arab seafarers, it became a key trading port of the Portuguese, was fortified by the Dutch, then became an administrative centre under the British, and today it is a palimpsest of superimposed layers of occupation (see photograph on page 25).

A graphic picture of life in the Kandyan Kingdom in the mid 17th century was given by an English seaman called Robert Knox who was held prisoner by the king of Kandy for almost 20 years (Knox, 1681): "Their houses are small, low, thatched Cottages, built with sticks, daubed with clay, the walls made very smooth..... The great people have handsom and commodious houses... commonly two buildings, one opposite each-other, joined on each side by a wall, which make a square courtyard in the middle.... Their furniture is but small.... a few earthen pots which hang up in slings.... a stool or two without backs."

Opposite: The Ecknelligoda *walauwe* at Kuruwita, ancestral home of the Mollamures, an ancient manor house rebuilt during the early 19th century.
Top: A typical village house of mud walls under a thatch roof surrounded by its home garden.
Above: A typical dry-zone house, its front verandah covered by deep overhanging eaves.

Right: A typical highland tea estate bungalow: the Kotyagala Estate, Bogowantalawa, built in the early 20th century.
Below: A typical low-country coconut estate bungalow: the Willigama Estate, Dankotuwa, built in the early 20th century.

The Portuguese created fortified settlements around the coast and lived in storied houses, their living quarters raised above their business premises. They introduced European furniture, shuttered windows and half-round clay tiles. The Dutch, for whom Sri Lanka was simply one link in a whole chain of Asian possessions, lived in single-storied courtyard houses with deep covered verandahs.

The British displaced the Dutch at the end of the 18th century and took control of the whole island, quickly turning large parts of it into vast plantations. To this end they created a comprehensive infrastructure of ports, roads and railways along with a range of functional and utilitarian buildings. They lived in detached houses which were referred to as 'bungalows'. These consisted, typically, of an arrangement of cellular rooms organised under a pitched roof with bay windows and covered verandas and stood, aloof, at the centre of a garden looking out towards an alien world. They came in all shapes and sizes and in a variety of eclectic styles.

The middle-class Sri Lankans of the burgeoning towns built their own localised versions of the British bungalow, while in the countryside the peasant-farmers continued to build in mud and thatch. During the Kandyan period only those close to the king were allowed to build with brick and tile, and local chieftains had to make do with larger versions of peasant houses. This changed during the 18th century when weakening central power and increasing European influence led to the emergence of a new style of manor house or *walauwe*. These were built of brick with white plastered Tuscan columns, clay-tiled roofs, carved wooden doors with elaborate fanlights, deep verandas and enclosed courtyards in what might be called the Porto-Sinhalese style. Such *walauwes* continued to be built well into the 19th century, but were later eclipsed by the houses of the new rich, men who had made their money from plumbago and arrack and who chose to advertise the wealth with ornate mansions, often copied from neighbouring India.

A number of British architectural firms were established in Colombo at the beginning of the 20th century. Typical were Edwards, Reid & Begg, the architects of the new Colombo Town Hall of 1926, who built a wide range of buildings — factories, hotels, public buildings, private houses — in a gamut of styles from Neo-Classical to Neo-Kandyan. These styles were copied by Sri Lankan house-builders in Colombo's growing suburbs.

Sri Lanka's first 'modern' houses were designed at the very end of the British period by tea-taster-turned-architect Andrew Boyd who set up a practice in Colombo in 1937. In the two years before the outbreak of World War II he built a handful of modern designs, including a startling house with a curving white facade on the hillside above Kandy Lake for art-lover Harold Pieris.

When Sri Lanka regained its independence in 1948 there were only about 20 qualified architects in the island and there was no professional body and no school of architecture.

In 1957 a group of 15 architects came together to form the Sri Lanka Institute of Architects (SLIA) and elected Oliver Weerasinghe, a graduate of Liverpool University, as their first president. The new Institute was modeled very much along the lines of the Royal Institute of British Architects in London, and in 1960 the parent institute granted it 'Allied Society' status.

The pioneer of architectural education in Sri Lanka was Justin Samarasekera, a graduate of the JJ School in Bombay who started a three-year architecture course in the Katubedde Technical College during the early 1960s. In 1973 the course was extended to five years, received RIBA recognition and became a part of the University of Moratuwa.

A second private school was opened in Colombo in 1986 under the aegis of the SLIA and offered a seven-year part-time course which later also attracted RIBA recognition.

One gauge of the success of the two schools is the fact that the SLIA now boasts around 1,000 members, the majority of whom have trained in Sri Lanka. The profession is well established and its registration procedures are fully recognised by government.

A pioneering architect of the post-independence period, Minnette de Silva was born in Kandy in 1918 and had the distinction of being the first Asian woman to be elected a member of the RIBA. She trained first in Mumbai but completed her studies at the AA in London. During this period she became a close friend of many leading architects of the day, including le Corbusier. Having qualified in 1948, she set up an office in her native Kandy.

Her house for the Karunaratne family, completed in 1950, achieved a precarious balance between tradition and modernity: the flow of space around the central open staircase was decidedly modern, though the plan was also tailored to accommodate traditional Buddhist ceremonies; the structure employed the latest techniques in reinforced concrete design but the building fabric incorporated local timber, rubble stone and traditional craftsmanship.

De Silva was involved with her sister Anil in the founding of *MARG*, a Mumbai-based magazine devoted to the arts and architecture. In 1953 the magazine carried her account of the Karunaratne house. This took the form of a manifesto for a Modern Regional Architecture – an architecture which would embrace modernity while still responding to place and to culture. This theoretical position predated the propositions of such luminaries as Frampton and Tzonis by about 30 years.

De Silva was active during the 1950s and 1960s and produced a number of innovative designs, but the fact that she was a woman in a male-dominated profession and was stuck in the provincial backwater of Kandy left her marginalised. In the 1970s she moved first to London and then to a teaching position in Hong Kong. Her later attempts to revive her Kandy practice during the 1980s were unsuccessful and she died, alone and forgotten, in 1998.

De Silva's natural successor and fellow pioneer was Geoffrey Bawa who was born in Colombo in 1919. Having first studied law in Britain he later qualified as architect at the AA in London, and in 1957 became a partner in the now moribund firm of Edwards, Reid & Begg.

Top: The Maurice and Malkanti Perera House, Alfred House Gardens, Colombo. Ulrik Plesner, 1962.
Middle: Pieris House I, Alfred House Gardens, Colombo. Minnette de Silva, 1952.
Bottom: Senanayake Apartments, Gregorys Road, Colombo. Minnette de Silva, 1957.

Top: The main sitting room/verandah of the architect's Colombo town house. Geoffrey Bawa, *circa* 1970.
Above: The central staircase of the Illangakoon House, Colombo. Valentine Gunasekara, 1969.

Soon after starting out in practice, Bawa recruited a young Danish architect called Ulrik Plesner who worked as his close associate for eight years. Although their early joint work conformed to the tenets of 'Tropical Modernism' — as promoted by Maxwell Fry and Jane Drew at the AA in London — they soon shifted towards a more regionalist approach.

In 1959 they produced a design for Dr A S H de Silva in Galle which broke up the house into its constituent parts and re-assembled them, pinwheel fashion, on a hillside under a single over-sailing roof. In the following year they built a town house for artist Ena de Silva in which the same parts were reassembled to form a central courtyard and a series of peripheral courtyards in the manner of a traditional *walauwe*, the very antithesis of a British Bungalow. Then in 1963 they built an estate bungalow at Polontalawa in which the main living space was defined only by a massive roof which spanned between two huge boulders. At the same time Plesner produced a trio of simple modern houses in what might be called a Scandinavian-Ceylonese mode. All of these designs asserted the importance of the roof as the primary element of a tropical house and all attempted to break down the barriers between inside and outside space, creating verandahs, open-to-the-sky courtyards and clear routes for cross ventilation.

Sri Lanka's third pioneer, Valentine Gunasekara, was born in 1931. Although 12 years younger than Bawa they were contemporaries at the AA School in London. Like Bawa, Gunasekara became a partner in the firm of Edwards, Reid & Begg, and the two shared the same office for ten years, though each had his own clients and assistants. As the decade drew on, however, their paths diverged. Gunasekara became pre-occupied with 'form-making', using in-situ concrete in an expressionist-modernist manner, while Bawa adopted a 'contemporary vernacular' position and sought inspiration from traditional technologies. In 1967 Gunasekara broke away to start his own office and Plesner returned to the UK leaving Bawa to set up a new partnership with engineer K Poologasundram.

Gunasekara's design for the Illangakoon House of 1969 was contained within a box, some 30 by 20 metres in plan and two storeys in height. Voids were carved out of this volume to create courtyards, roof terraces and lightwells which were screened with pergolas and grilles. Spaces within the box were defined by free-standing screens and changes in level. On the ground floor there was a continuous flow of space from the open car port to the sitting and dining spaces. At its centre a grand spiral staircase accentuated the flow of space and corkscrewed up to the bedrooms and family spaces of the first floor.

Gunasekara's most significant buildings were designed for the Catholic Church and he built an innovative hotel at Tangalla in 1970. But he also produced a series of radical houses culminating in an expressionist fantasy at Mount Lavinia in 1987. But by then his practice had petered out and in the same year he moved to a teaching position in the United States. Few of his houses survive, though his influence on future generations has been considerable.

Bawa managed to survive the lean years of the early 1970s. In 1969 he had converted a row of tiny cottages off Bagatelle Road into a town house for himself, creating a hybrid design which combined courtyard and tower typologies and served as a test bed for his evolving ideas. In 1973 he applied his innovative ideas to the design of a row of four courtyard houses and in 1977 he built a radically minimalist four-storey tower house for the Martenstyn family.

1977 saw the election of a new government and, in quick succession, Bawa landed the two biggest commissions of his career — the design of a new parliament in the Colombo suburb of Kotte and the masterplan of a new university near Matara.

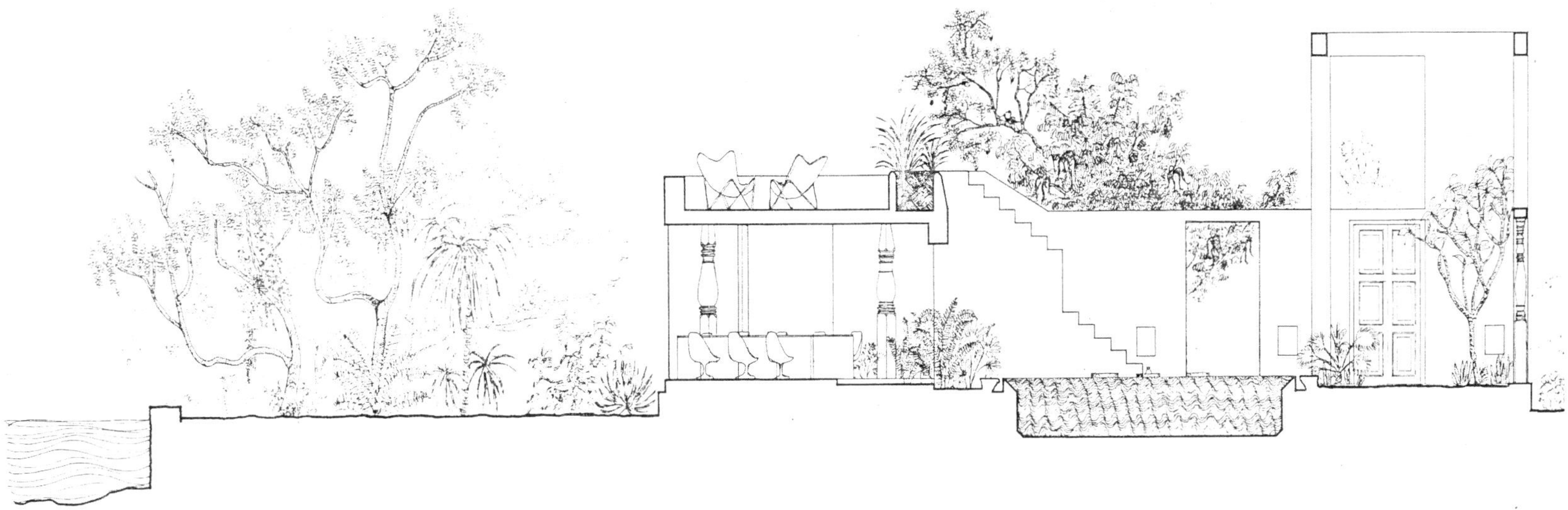

After 1980 a number of big practices emerged, among them Design Group 5, The Design Consortium, Mihindu Keerthiratne Associates, Surath Wickramasinghe Associates and Tanya and Suren Wickremasinghe Architects. These were all run along modern lines and produced predominantly commercial and administrative buildings, usually in the modern global idiom.

During the 1960s, Bawa had built up a core of talented assistants, though after 1970 these left him, one by one, to pursue their own careers and became leading members of the second generation of Sri Lankan architects.

Turner Wickramasinghe, one of Bawa's first assistants, was appointed chief architect in the State Engineering Corporation and in 1980 produced the masterplan for the new town of Seeduwa Raddoluwa.

Pheroze Choksy and Ismeth Raheem started a joint practice in 1976 and went on to design a range of commercial and hotel projects, including the celebrated Lodge Hotel at Habarana.

Anura Ratnavibhushana, who had been one of Bawa's closest collaborators, spent periods as a partner in Design Group Five and as an associate of Mihindu Keerthiratne, but continued to work independently. In 1982 he designed a magical house for himself on a remote spit of land at Lunava, south of Colombo. This was widely illustrated (Powell, 1996) and became an icon of modern design in the tropics.

Vasantha Jacobson had been Bawa's project architect for the new Parliament but she quit in 1986 and retired to a Buddhist monastery in the hills. She had worked on a number of Bawa's house projects, but is best remembered for the tiny walled house that she and her Danish husband built in Havelock Town in the mid 1970s.

Mention should also be made of C Anjalendran who worked briefly for Bawa at the end of the 1970s but continued to act as his unpaid assistant for a further ten years, while running his own office on his mother's verandah. Anjalendran produces robust designs which use rugged local materials and emphasises the need for adequate shade and good ventilation. He is best known for the series of schools and orphanages which he built for SOS Childrens' Villages, but he has also designed a steady stream of private houses.

Top: Section through the architect's own house at Lunava. Anura Ratnavibhushana, 1982. Drawing by Anura Ratnvibhushana.
Above: House on the Red Cliffs at Mirissa. Geoffrey Bawa, 1997.

Top: The House Beneath the Banyan Tree, Colombo. C Anjalendran, 2002.
Above: Central court at the Mount Cinnamon Estate Bungalow. C Anjalendran, 2004.
Opposite: Aerial view of the Galle Fort. The fort has been in continuous occupation for at least 1,000 years and shows signs of Arab, Portuguese, Dutch and British settlement.

At the end of the 1980s Geoffrey Bawa withdrew from Edwards, Reid & Begg and opened a small design studio with a group of young assistants that included Sumangala Jayatilleke, Amila de Mel and Channa Daswatte. Together they embarked on a decade of feverish activity, producing designs for an astonishing trio of hotels and a final series of innovative houses. These latter included a minimalist pavilion for Pradeep Jayawardene on the Red Cliffs overlooking Weligama Bay in 1997. In 1998 a stroke effectively ended Bawa's career and he died five years later in 2003.

Since his death, Bawa's estate has been managed by a group of collaborators and friends who have succeeded in preserving his garden at Lunuganga and opening up his Colombo town house to the public. They also organise a triennial award for architecture which has showcased the work of a new generation of architects.

During the 65 years since independence, Sri Lanka's population has tripled from seven to over 20 million. Much of these increases have taken place in urban areas — villages have become towns and towns have grown into cities.

The capital, Colombo, is still officially defined as occupying the boundaries of the original British municipality but in reality it stretches out like an amoeba across surrounding countryside and is now home to more than three million people. Much of Colombo's growth has been unplanned and its infrastructure is antiquated. This has created a dearth of land suitable for development and exacerbated the shortage of affordable housing.

In the late 1970s there was a determined attempt by the government to instigate effective city planning and to solve the housing problem with a comprehensive building programme. Five new satellite towns were built around the capital and the parliament was moved from the old city centre to a new site at Kotte, some ten kilometres to the east. Ambitious plans for a new capital city to be built around the parliament came to nothing and a subsequent land-rush resulted in the uncontrolled growth of congested suburbs at Kotte and Battaramulla.

The completion of the new parliament coincided with the onset of the civil war in the north and the east and directed minds and money away from problems of housing and planning. Economic uncertainty brought public housing projects almost to a standstill and discouraged the formation of a functioning housing market. Condominiums have, until recently, been relatively uncommon — prices are pitched beyond the pocket of many locals and buyers tend to be foreigners and expatriate Sri Lankans. As a result middle class families have been forced to take matters into their own hands and build houses for themselves, often on small un-serviced plots.

This has brought a flood of commissions for young architects and architect-designed houses are now much more common in Sri Lanka than in many parts of the world. As a result, a new generation of architects has become adept at producing innovative designs with tight budgets on small plots, building inward-looking houses, which function as oases of calm shut off from the increasingly chaotic urban environment that surrounds them.

The Sri Lankan architects whose work is represented in this book belong primarily to the third post-independence generation. Most of them were born between 1962 and 1972, and all have pursued at least a part of their architectural studies in Sri Lanka. Four of them worked as assistants to Geoffrey Bawa and seven have worked in the office of Anjalendran.

All the signs are that the efforts of the early pioneers have borne fruit. A diverse tradition of contemporary Sri Lankan architecture now exists and the designs of Sri Lankan architects can be shown alongside those of eminent international practitioners like Tadao Ando, Shigeru Ban and Kerry Hill. Sri Lanka is a relatively small country, one sixtieth of the size of its nearest neighbour, but in the field of architecture it punches well above its weight.

Bawa's Legacy: The Horagolla Stables

David Robson

During a career which spanned from 1957 to 1997, Geoffrey Bawa established himself as the most significant Sri Lankan architect of his day. This present survey of contemporary houses in Sri Lanka has focused on a new generation of architects, most of them born some 50 years after Bawa, but it has revealed that many of them have been influenced by him in one way or another, consciously or unconsciously.

That influence, however, does not reveal itself in a style – 'Bawa Style' exists only in the minds of magazine writers, estate agents and what Alexander Pope referred to as 'imitating fools'. Bawa himself was continually experimenting and never repeated himself. For him the idea of style was anathema. Every new commission was a challenge, a new problem which demanded a new solution. What he bequeathed was a particular way of seeing, or what he himself described as 'a way of building'. For him this entailed embracing the new while learning from the past, selecting appropriate materials and construction techniques, playing with light and shade, creating a scenographic sequence of linked and interlocking spaces, breaking down the barriers between inside and outside, designing with the landscape.

Bawa will be remembered principally for his major public buildings such as the new Sri Lanka Parliament at Kotte and the Ruhunu University campus at Matara and for his masterly series of hotels. But he also designed over 50 private houses in Sri Lanka of which about 40 were actually built. These ranged from a first house for Preeni Deraniyagala in Guilford Crescent, commissioned whilst he was still a reluctant lawyer and built soon after he qualified as an architect, to a last house for Pradeep Jayawardene on the Red Cliffs at Mirissa which was completed shortly before he suffered his final stroke. This canon of designs altered the perceptions of a whole generation of Sri Lankan city dwellers and helped to set in motion a lifestyle revolution. Sadly many of his houses have now been altered beyond recognition and several have been demolished. Only a handful survive today in their original state to bear witness to the genius of their creator.

Bawa's remodelling of an old stable block at Horagolla for Sunethra Bandaranaike marks the mid-point of his career and is one design which survives intact. Sunethra was a close friend and to this day remains a leading member of the Geoffrey Bawa Trust. When she first approached him 1983 he was reluctant to take on the project, but all of his misgivings evaporated when they visited the site together. Having set out her requirements Sunethra gave him a freehand and he worked on the project for four years with his assistant Philip Fowler.

The main house or *walauwe* at Horagolla was built by Sunethra's great-grandfather and tradition has it that its stable block was fashioned out of an older house which had been occupied by earlier generations of the family. This would explain how the Bandaranaike horses came to be lodged in such an elegant neo-classical structure. The building lies beyond the northern corner of

Top: The southeast elevation of the former stables.
Above: View from the main lawn through the former stables.
Opposite: Original drawings include the long section running from northeast to southwest through the former stables (above) and (below) a general plan. The proposed swimming pool was never built.

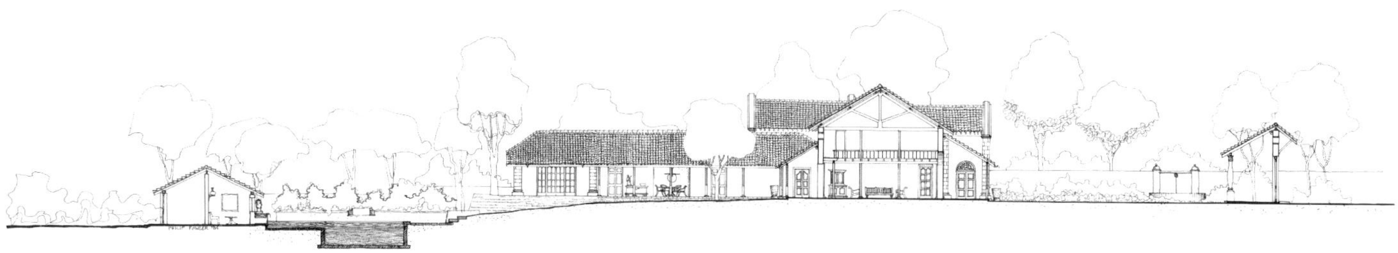

SECTION

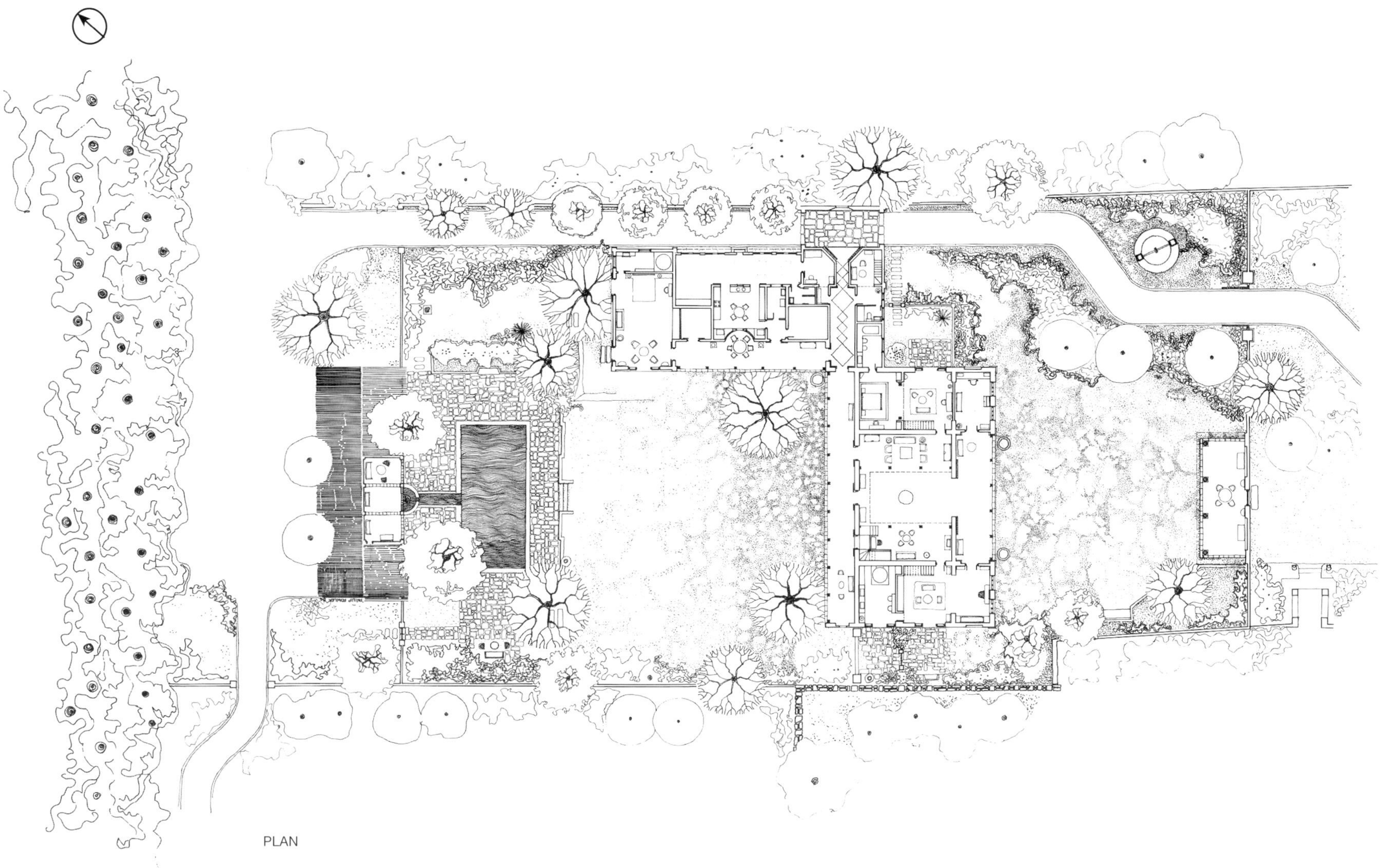

PLAN

the main house and faces towards the magnificent stand of *hora* trees that gave the estate its name.

Bawa established generous garden courts to either side of the stable block, enclosing them within high screen walls. A new wing containing the dining verandah, the kitchens and a guest suite was projected from the north corner of the stables along the northeast edge of the rear lawn to create an L-shaped ensemble. A neo-classical *porte cochère* was then inserted at the elbow between the two wings to line up axially with a long verandah which was added behind the blank back wall of the stable block. Finally a line of garages and staff rooms was placed along the far edge of the lawn to form a foil against the backdrop of *hora* trees.

All of these changes allowed Bawa to sidestep an obvious full-frontal entrance sequence. Instead he created a spiral loop, smuggling visitors past the side of the main house and along a walled alley to the new *porte cochère*. From there they traverse the cross axis of the long verandah, encountering the dining verandah and the rear lawn, before arriving at the central axis of the composition to discover the main stable hall and beyond it, like a secret garden, the front lawn.

The stable hall has been fashioned into a double-height living space with a timber mezzanine added to give scale and articulation. Its two flanks were then given over to the principle bedrooms and the library.

The two garden courts function like a pair of grand open-to-the-sky rooms and the life of the house takes place on the various verandahs that line their edges. This makes the magnificent stable hall seem almost superfluous — like Bawa's own sitting room at Lunuganga its main purpose is to act as a link between verandahs or to provide shelter from the monsoon.

The conversion was achieved with great restraint, a restraint which has been echoed in the choice of furniture and artworks. But Bawa could not resist adding in a few witticisms — the two occuli which mark the ends of the long verandah, the ancient fan which hangs from a gallows' bracket above the dining table, the name boards of long-deceased horses, the loggia on the front lawn with the door which leads nowhere, and the art deco bathrooms which seem to have escaped from a Hollywood movie.

Horagolla is not one of Bawa's most revolutionary designs but it is one of his most accomplished. He treated an ancient building with respect, adding a new chapter to its unfolding story, and he created an elegant pleasure pavilion for a cherished friend.

Opposite, from left to right: Archway detail; column detail; the occulus in the *porte cochère*.
Above: The sitting room in the former stables.
Right: The staircase up to the mezzanine.
Far right: A corner of the main verandah.
Overleaf: The stunning view of the Indian Ocean from the terrace of the Kadju House at Tangalla designed by Pradeep Kodikara. The house was the recipient of the 2014 Geoffrey Bawa Award.

Guava House

Mawanella

Architect	Ranjan Aluwihare *RA Designs*

The Guava House is the romantic weekend retreat of Sri Lankan architect Ranjan Aluwihare (48), his Anglo-Irish wife Shaunagh and their two teenage offspring, currently at university and school in the UK. The family visits the house once a month from their home in Colombo. The architect, a descendent of a distinguished Kandyan family, was born in Putney, London. At that time, his father was the head of the Civil Engineering Department at the Greater London Council (GLC). Aluwihare's grand-father's brother was the celebrated civil servant and diplomat Sir Richard Aluwihare. Aluwihare recounts meeting Geoffrey Bawa in 1979, when he was 13 years old. "There was a hugely creative spirit in the air," he recalls, "with Bawa, his brother Bevis Bawa, Barbara Sansoni and Laki Senanayake all doing wonderful things. I remember my father's advice — don't become an architect!"

Nevertheless, Aluwihare studied fine art and interior design at the Chelsea School of Art in London and architecture at the North London Polytechnic School of Architecture, now the University of North London, and he graduated in 1985. He then worked in London with various architectural practices for more than a decade on a number of high profile projects that included a private residence for David Bowie, another for Lord Rothschild in Berkeley Square and yet another for Paul Getty in New York. He is now the Design Director of RA Designs specialising in restoration and interior design. He met his wife whose mother's family hails from County Waterford in Ireland, in London and they moved to Colombo in 1999. The site, a 1.4 hectare rubber plantation at Mawanella near Kegalle some 100 km northeast of the capital was purchased in 2005 and the Guava House was completed atop a hill in 2008.

The house is approached on foot via a steep climb from the west to an entrance verandah. Looking back one can see Bible Rock in the distance. The entrance lobby is on a central axis, flanked by two bedroom cores and one passes beneath a mezzanine floor to emerge in a soaring double-height living and dining area with timber folding doors that open to a broad timber pool deck and an infinity pool at the level of the tree canopy. A timber pergola shades the deck. A vehicle track is below the line of sight to the east of the pool and gives access to two guest pavilions — Mangosteen and Rambutan — named, like the house itself, after fruits that grow on the estate. They are located on the lower slopes with views of paddy fields.

The house is constructed with a steel frame, white painted fair-faced brick internal walls, teak beams and stairs, and mango hardwood timber cladding, with a roof of *iluk*, a reed obtained from Anaradapura that through a process of transpiration keeps the house

Previous page: The living room and kitchen extend out to a timber-decked verandah with views to the east over paddy fields. The pitched roof is clad with *iluk*, a grass from Anaradapura. **Opposite:** The infinity pool running adjacent the house is fringed by trees. **Right:** A view from the mezzanine level. The soaring living and breakfast area is naturally ventilated.

cool. Floors are timber throughout and there is a plank of deciduous hickory wood above the door. Ironwood is also used in the construction. Air-conditioning is unnecessary and the house is naturally ventilated with air movement assisted by ceiling fans. In the morning the sun rises over the infinity pool and mist hangs in the lower branches of the trees. The glazed upper gable of the house allows sunlight to filter to the interior.

Aluwihare is also an accomplished artist who has exhibited at the Barefoot Gallery in Colombo and several of his beautiful watercolours hang in the house. The architect's wife, who acted as client, coordinated the soft furnishings in the house and two pavilions. Explaining their affection for the house and its location she describes it as a "21st-century Huckleberry Finn house". She continues, "We love it when we are here when it is windy and raining; living in a house like this in an April thunderstorm is great fun."

The tranquil setting of the house provides an ideal ambience for meditation and the house and two pavilions are in demand as a venue for residential yoga classes of up to eight people. Kundalini Yoga teacher training workshops and Scaravelli inspired yoga retreats attract participants from far afield to immerse themselves in yoga, holistic food and light exercise in a jungle setting.

The Guava House was built in collaboration with the architect's cousin Rohan Aluwihare, also an architect, and in January 2014 they were both shortlisted for a Geoffrey Bawa Award. The architects have also carried out the restoration and interior design of a number of historic houses within the walls of Galle Fort that are popular vacation destinations.

Opposite: The living area is shaded from the morning sun by a timber pergola over the verandah. Air movement is assisted by ceiling fans.
Top right: The house sits atop a hill. The entrance is reached by a steep flight of stairs.
Centre right: Timber folding doors permit a direct connection between interior and exterior.
Right: A view along the verandah from the outdoor dining area beneath the pergola.
Overleaf: The house viewed from the lower vehicle access track.

SECTION

GROUND FLOOR PLAN

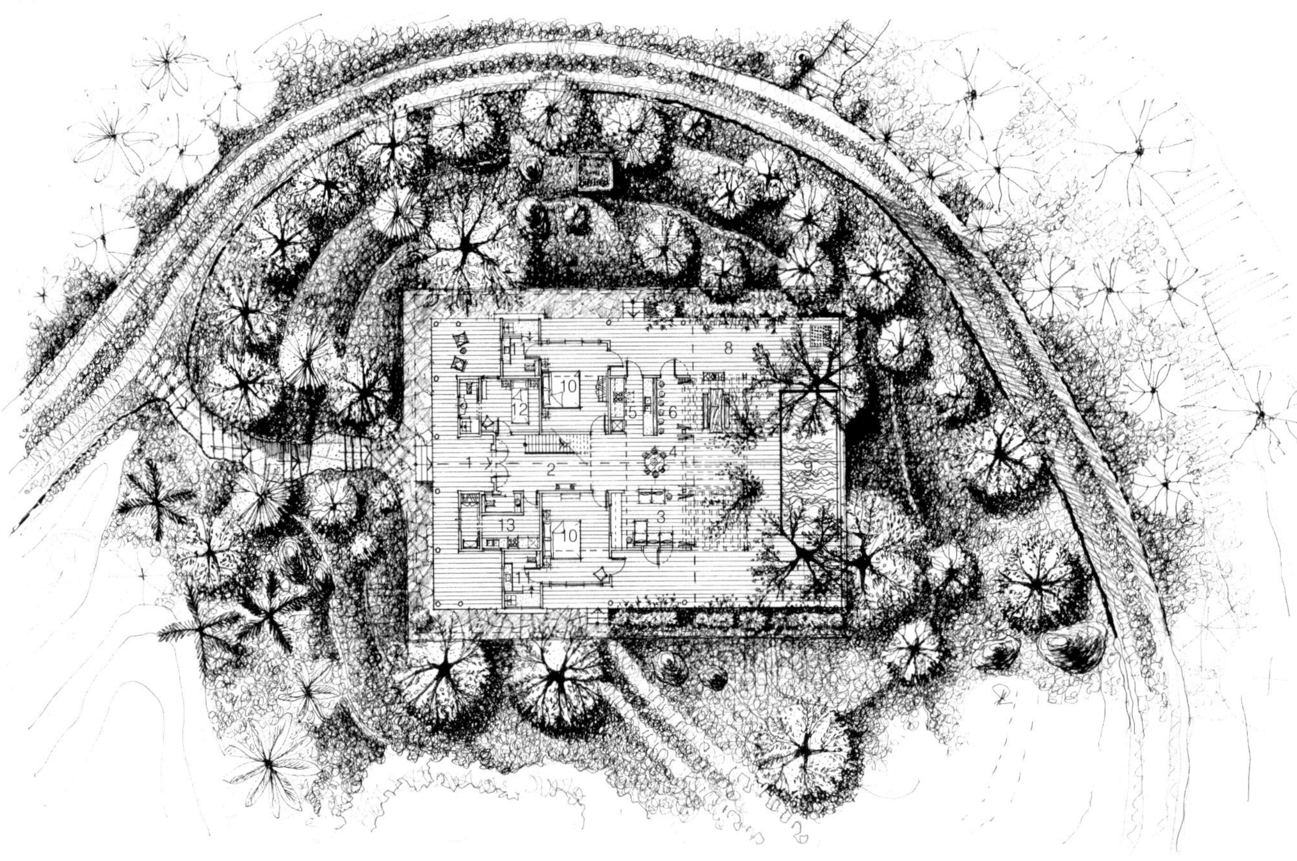

1	Entrance	8	Verandah
2	Hall	9	Pool
3	Living	10	Bedroom
4	Breakfast	11	Bathroom
5	Kitchen	12	Guest Bedroom
6	Bar	13	Laundry
7	Dining		

Kalundewa Retreat

Dambulla

Architect Sanath Liyanage
SLA Architects

The Kalandewa Retreat is an enchanting villa set in an idyllic landscape at Dambulla, 148 km north of Colombo. The site is approached by a narrow red gravel track through lush green paddy fields encompassed by picturesque mountains. Originally designed as a modern house at the heart of a 40-hectare (100-acre) estate growing a wide variety of rice, fruit and vegetables, the house is now the centre of a thriving boutique retreat with the addition of several outlying chalets.

The original house has a rectangular plan form, with the longer sides facing east and west. Entered from the south, initially along a gravel path through an orchard and then via a timber walkway, one passes a small store and pantry to arrive at a timber deck beneath a wide overhanging roof. Sliding folding doors give access to a soaring double-height living/dining space

that is wonderfully light and spacious with an open riser staircase ascending to the upper level. The living area looks west to a small man-made irrigation lake fringed by mangrove.

To the rear of the staircase and facing east across verdant green paddy field is the principal bedroom with a dressing room and ensuite bathroom. Beyond the dining space, through more sliding folding doors, is another broad timber deck, this one facing north, with a plunge pool and a timber jetty extending out over the lake. At the upper level is a second large east-facing bedroom with ensuite facilities and a roof deck that spans over the service rooms for family barbecues. The minimalistic detailing of the steel structure, fair faced brick walls, off form concrete and teak joinery is of the highest quality and a perfect foil for the surrounding natural habitat.

The architect of the retreat is Sanath Liyanage (43), a graduate of the City School of Architecture in Colombo (1995–2002). His most influential teachers were Channa Daswatte, Madhura Prematilleke and Hiranti Welandawe and, while studying, he worked for Prematilleke and Welandawe. Upon gaining his practice license in 2004 he set up SLA Architects.

Completed in 2009, the Kalundewa Retreat is essentially a glass box with a simple north-facing mono pitch roof where the intention is that from any point within the house one can be in touch with nature — either literally by venturing out onto the verandah or by visual contact from within the house. The steel and glass box might be uncomfortably hot in the late afternoon were it not for a thick grove of *kumbuk* trees and the hardwood *mila* trees that surround the house

Previous page: The steel-framed pavilion is elevated on concrete piles. A north-facing timber deck extends out from the living area.
Opposite: The house is essentially a glass box that relies upon existing mature trees to prevent excessive solar heat gain.
Right: The living area is a stunning double-height space.

and mitigate the effects of insolation. The perimeter glazing opens to the natural environment and permits cross ventilation.

It is a stunning location and the owners have built upon its natural assets, growing much of the produce consumed by guests in its own sustainably farmed paddy fields, vegetable gardens and fruit orchards using traditional Sri Lankan farming methods. Guests can visit the agricultural activities or arrange for collection by a raft to view the aquatic wildlife in the man-made irrigation lakes. The profusion of wildlife is a major attraction to visitors with hornbills, egrets, peacocks and myriad smaller birds attracted to the 'oasis'. A short walk from the house is an *ulpotha* or fresh water spring — perfect for a relaxing bathe in crystal clear water.

Just two kilometres from the house and studio of the artist Laki Senanayake, the retreat is magical in the evening as lights reflect in the still waters of the lake and frogs begin a refrain. Mornings, too, are breath-taking as the sun rises over the misty paddy fields.

Above: A jetty projects over the surrounding man-made lake fringed by mangrove vegetation. A raft affords access to appreciate the lake's abundant wildlife.
Right: The surrounding vegetation embraces the house providing a constant connection with nature.

Above left: The entrance to the house is via a red gravel track and a short timber bridge.

Above right: The sun deck facing due north is an extension of the interior living area.

Opposite top: The master bedroom suite with a rooftop deck beyond.

Opposite bottom: An elegant steel and timber open-riser staircase gives access to the upper floor.

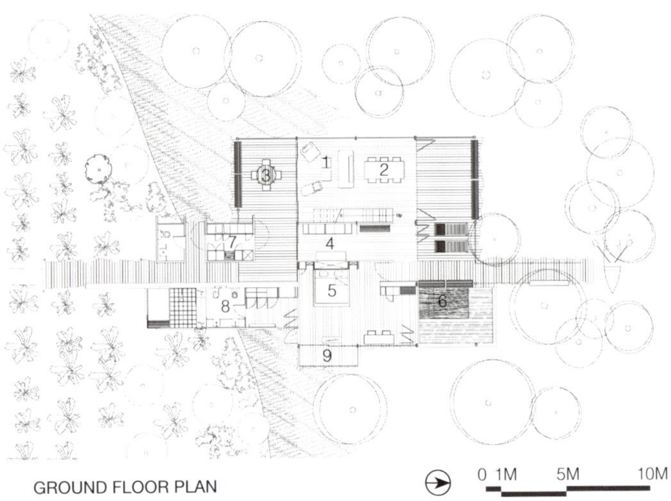

GROUND FLOOR PLAN

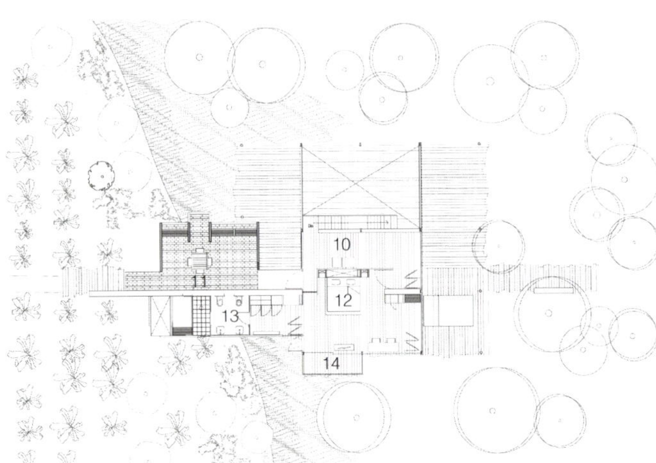

FIRST FLOOR PLAN

1	Living	8	Bathroom / WC
2	Dining	9	Balcony
3	Verandah	10	Lounge
4	Library	11	Rooftop Lounge
5	Bedroom	12	Bedroom
6	Jacuzzi	13	Bathroom / WC
7	Kitchen & Pantry	14	Balcony

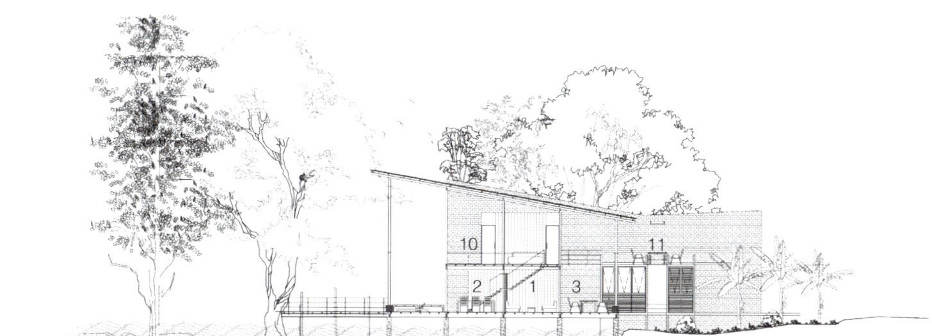

SECTION

Above: The walled courtyard has four rows of geometrically arranged trees that are juxtaposed against the openness and wildness of the lakeside garden.
Right: The house is set back from the shore of Bolgoda Lake. A jetty fashioned from recycled ironwood railway sleepers extends over the water.
Opposite: The public façade reveals little of the exclusive private space within

Villa 14

Ruskin Island

Architect Waruna Gomis
I W Associates

Villa 14 is located 15 kilometres south of Colombo on secluded Ruskin Island and is reached by a utilitarian two-car ferry across the Bolgoda Lake. The house was designed initially as a home for a businessman and his family. Subsequently, it has been promoted as a guest villa — an idyllic hideaway to escape the hectic life of the inner city.

The architect of the house is Waruna Gomis (37) who is also an acclaimed architectural photographer. Educated at Mahanama College and the City School of Architecture, Colombo, Gomis graduated in 2003 and became a registered architect in 2004. He worked with Geoffrey Bawa as an architectural assistant from 1997 to 2000 on a proposed Presidential Palace, extensions to the Kandalama Hotel and a house for Jai Metha in Mumbai. In 2009 he was the photographer for a monograph of the work of architect C Anjalendran.[1]

In 2011 Gomis set up his own practice I W Associates with a long-time friend Indika Samarasinghe. The practice has found a niche in the design of low-energy industrial buildings and it is currently involved in projects which are based upon LEED certification systems.

Villa 14 was completed in 2012 and is designed as a series of dramatic spatial experiences along a linear route on a north south axis. Entering through a pair of heavy purposely-rusted steel doors set in a high stone wall, one progresses north towards a gap in a second stone wall directly ahead. To the west is a glazed pavilion with two guest bedrooms and open-to-sky bathrooms entered via a bridge across a koi pond. The pavilion has an intriguing Japanese character. To the east is a delightful al-fresco dining court with a compact kitchenette and service area.

Arriving at the gap in the wall, two steps down gives access into a rectangular paved, walled courtyard with an avenue of 12 *karanda* trees leading to a two-storey pavilion, set across the axis. The pavilion is open at ground-floor level with the two bedrooms at the upper level overlooking the lake and accessed by an open-sided stair to the right.

To the north of the pavilion is an infinity lap pool and beyond the pool a lawn sloping gently to the reeds that border the lake. A timber jetty of ironwood railway sleepers extends out above the mantle of lotus flowers that cover the fringe of the lake, to a sitting place on the jetty that terminates the 'journey'.

Retracing one's steps, one notices two towers in the walled courtyard — one supporting the water storage tank, the other giving access to a third bedroom in the guest pavilion. "The weight of the water tank necessitated a steel frame structure to support it so we decided to have symmetrical structures," Gomis explains.

The spatial sequence is brilliantly conceived — it is inward looking until the final vista is revealed and thoroughly beguiling. When discussing Villa 14, Gomis is open in his praise of his former employers. "Bawa influenced me, he pushed me and gave me confidence," he states. "In this design, the plan is very clear and undiluted, the sequence of entry and progression through the house is clear."

"But I learned this from Arosha Perera of Milroy Perera Associates, the idea of a sequence of spaces, of discovery, of the different quality of spaces," continues Gomis. When asked about other influences, he mentions he has acquired the monographs of Singapore-based architects, Kerry Hill and Ernesto Bedmar, whose work he admires.

"The living space in the pavilion now has sliding glass doors on the façade facing the lake,' Gomis explains, "whereas originally the living area was much more open to the pool and the lake. But there were concerns about snakes and the like, so a screen was added." In fact, the concerns may be well founded for, even as we photographed the house, a 1.5 m long monitor lizard ambled across the lawn by the water's edge followed by a smaller companion. For visitors interested in photographing wildlife, the house is a marvelous venue: in the course of a day one can also view porcupines, egrets, kingfishers and a host of small birds.

[1] Robson, David, *Anjalendran: Architect of Sri Lanka*, Tuttle, Singapore, 2009.

Opposite: The jetty leads to a quiet place for contemplation and appreciation of nature.
Above left: A simple concrete staircase ascends to the master bedroom suite.
Above right: The parking court precedes a dramatic spatial sequence behind the door.
Right: A processional route leads from the entrance past the dining court and guest bedrooms to the inner courtyard.

Above left: An elegant guest bedroom with soft furnishings juxtaposed against stone and polished cement floors.
Above right: The shaded al- fresco dining court.
Opposite: The view from the living area to the central walled courtyard.

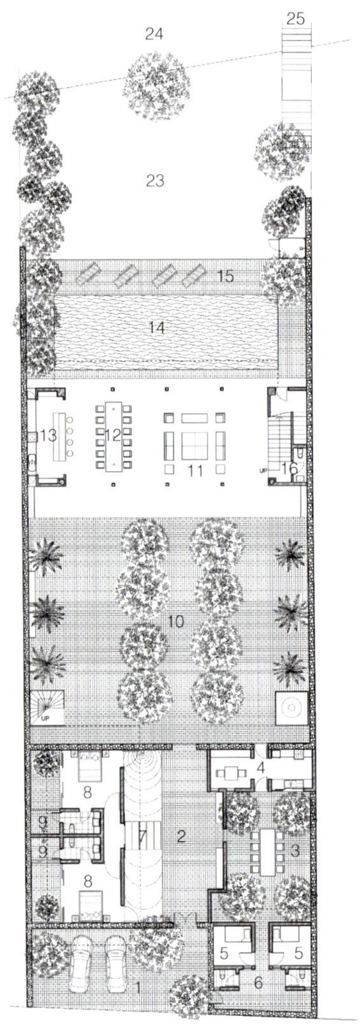

GROUND FLOOR PLAN

0 1M 5M 10M

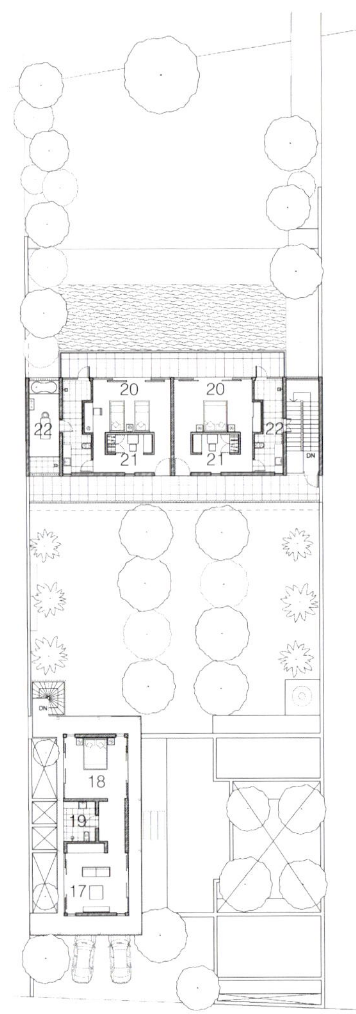

FIRST FLOOR PLAN

1 Carpark
2 Entrance
3 Dining Court
4 Kitchen
5 Staffroom
6 Staff Court / WC
7 Bridge
8 Guest Bedroom
9 Guest Bathroom
10 Courtyard
11 Living
12 Dining
13 Bar
14 Swimming Pool
15 Pool Deck
16 Powder Room
17 Guest Lounge
18 Guest Bedroom
19 Guest Bathroom
20 Bedroom
21 Dressing Room
22 Bathroom
23 Garden
24 Lake
25 Jetty

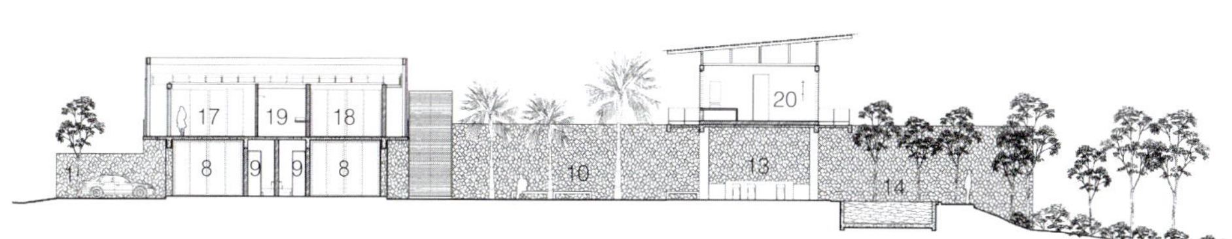

SECTION

Above: The central courtyard with guest suite to the left and the lap pool beyond. The original plantation bungalow is to the right.
Right: Two guest rooms share a sitting area alongside a perforated wall that provides natural ventilation.
Opposite: The original plantation bungalow has exhilarating views to the north. The façade has changed little since 1820.

Armitage Hill

Galle

Architect **Kerry Hill**
Kerry Hill Architects

Armitage Hill[1] is the vacation home of Singapore-based Australian architect Kerry Hill and his family. Located to the northeast of Galle, it served as a plantation manager's bungalow from 1820 onwards. The plantation owners had sited the house for pragmatic reasons so that the resident manager would be able to keep a watchful eye on the estate and the weather. The north facing verandah has exhilarating views to the horizon and it is said that on a clear day one can see as far as Adam's Peak. Between 1840 and 1880, ownership transferred into the hands of the Ephraim family who were the proprietors of the New Oriental Hotel in Galle Fort. In 1981, Hill and his wife Ruth chanced upon the property while on vacation in Sri Lanka and 12 years later they acquired it. Hill was attracted to Sri Lanka by his admiration for Geoffrey Bawa whom he had met in Bali in 1973.

When I first visited the house in the late 1990s Hill had made modest alterations to the bungalow. He is a tall man and, finding the internal height of the rooms excessively low, he raised the roof. He also removed some internal partitions to create an elegantly proportioned long gallery/living room across the axis of the house with two bedrooms to either side of the entrance hall served by new bathrooms. The kitchen and staff quarters were about 30 metres south of the house along with a water tower.

When I returned in February 2014 after a lapse of 14 years, dramatic changes had taken place. The simple bungalow and its environs had been transformed to create a spacious retreat. A guest pavilion with two Aman-style rooms and ensuite bathrooms stretches along the western boundary of the site; the lowly kitchen has morphed into an open sided dining pavilion with an adjacent remodeled kitchen, staff accommodation and service buildings; and, in 2007, the so-called Black Pavilion was added alongside the eastern access. A 20-metre blue-green lap pool has been 'dropped in' to the west of the old bungalow together with an elegant south-facing pool pavilion and a sun deck.

The additions are arrayed around a large open court just below the summit of the hill, and the whole dynamic of the house I visited more than a decade earlier has been altered dramatically. Previously, activities were orientated solely to the north from the verandah. Now, the life of the owners revolves around the court to the south of the old bungalow, and the pool terrace. Remarkably, the 'centre of gravity' has shifted.

Each of the pavilions that bound the court sits on a 'platform' and the slight difference in level between these platforms is negotiated by broad flights of stairs. The groundscape is a mixture of stone paving, red gravel and reed beds while two huge trees have been left undisturbed by the changes and provide welcome shade. In effect the space is a large 'outdoor room' measuring some 30m x 50m. Ficus plants cover the stone walls forming a green base. The dining pavilion with its 5m long polished cement table has become the primary focus and the meeting place for family and guests. There is a supply of umbrellas — they are a necessity during the monsoon season when one crosses the courtyard.

The major new addition is the Black Pavilion sitting to the southeast of the original bungalow and alongside the entrance. It is the first building encountered after leaving one's vehicle and ascending the gentle gradient. At the upper level of the two-storey pavilion there is an open-plan reception area and a living area. At the lower floor level there is a master bedroom, an en-suite bathroom and an outdoor terrace. Louvered black windows provide natural ventilation and the furniture is exclusively black. The pavilion looks south east to an area of tall slender palm trees. Hill describes the living space as "a garden room perched high among the palms.

Above left: Grassed terraces ascend along the east side of the original plantation bungalow.
Above right: The pool pavilion is reflected in the shimmering blue lap pool.
Opposite top: The Black Pavilion, the most recent addition to the hilltop complex, completes the sense of enclosure of the central courtyard.
Opposite below left: The kitchen/dining pavilion is a gathering point for family and guests.
Opposite below right: The central courtyard with its shallow platforms, steps, reed bed and mature trees has become the new focus of the complex.

Above: The east facing terrace and pond alongside the Black Pavilion
Left: The reception/living area of the Black Pavilion looking east.
Opposite top: A place for quiet contemplation in the guest pavilion.
Opposite bottom: Steps ascending from the pool terrace to the lawn.
Overleaf left: The gallery space in the original plantation bungalow.
Overleaf right: Sunrise is seen over the Black Pavilion.

The black interior is seen in silhouette and frames the view. Each opening is a different painting. One feels close to nature here, squirrels twitter, monkeys are curious and storms come and go. The sleeping space is more enclosed, protective, and opens to the morning light."[2] Hill has used the house as a test bed for materials and details he has incorporated in projects elsewhere.

In the asymmetric orthogonal composition the estate bungalow still forms the 'centrepiece', but its functions have devolved to the additional pavilions added over a period of 20 years. The reincarnation is a magical place where one can find places for solitude, silence and contemplation.

In a career spanning over 30 years Kerry Hill has carved out a special place in the development of architecture in Asia and beyond. His completed projects are a byword for quality and his work has inspired several young architects in this book. He has garnered numerous international awards including the Aga Khan Award for Architecture (2001) and the Royal Australian Institute of Architects Gold Medal (2006). Armitage Hill is extraordinarily handsome as one would expect from the home of an architect who has designed several of Asia's finest buildings.

[1] Powell, Robert, "Escape from the City" in SPACE 2000/04, Panpac Media, Singapore, 2000, p 74-77.
[2] Hill, Kerry, 'Armitage Hill', in *Crafting Modernism,* Thames and Hudson, London, 2013, p 384.

THE BLACK PAVILION — SECTION

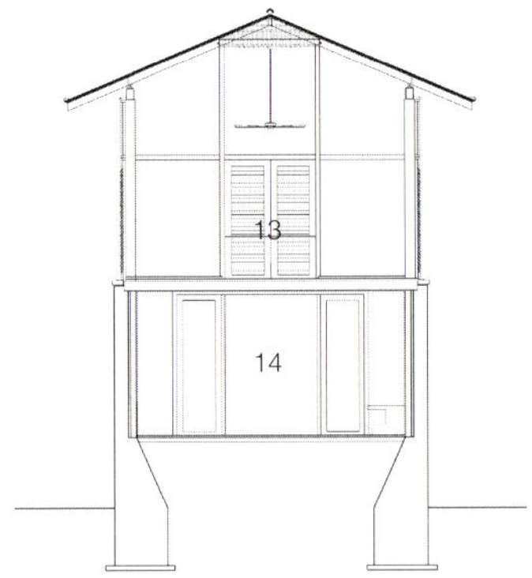

SITE PLAN

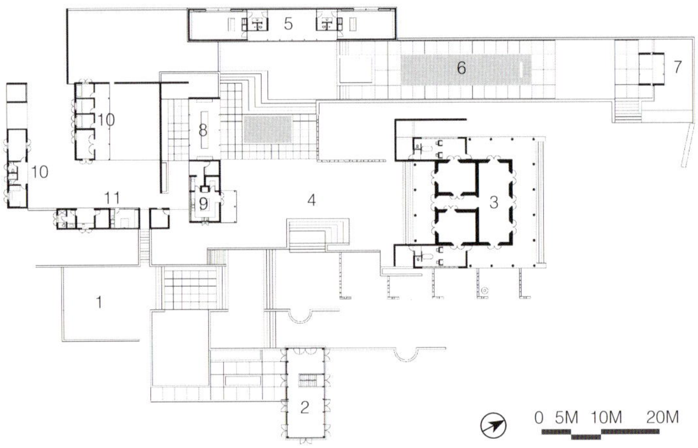

THE GUEST PAVILION — SECTION

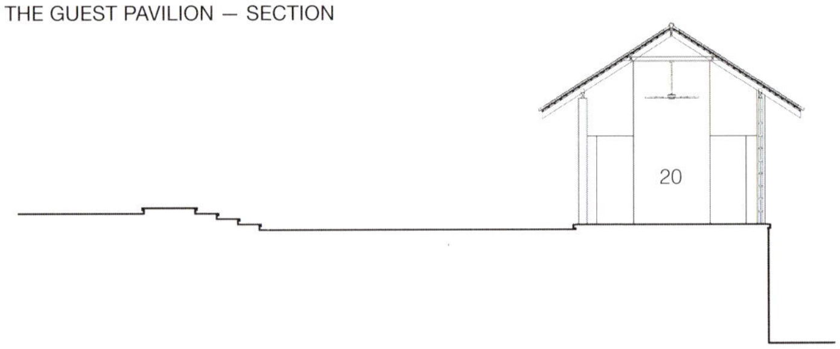

THE BLACK PAVILION — GROUND & FIRST FLOOR PLAN

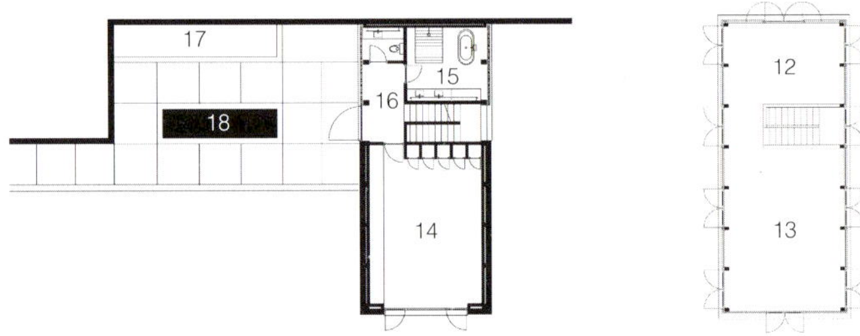

1	Drop Off	11	Service Block
2	Black Pavilion	12	Pavilion Entry
3	Main House	13	Living
4	Courtyard	14	Bedroom
5	Guest Pavilion	15	Bathroom
6	Swimming Pool	16	Lower Entry
7	Pool Pavilion	17	Planter
8	Dining	18	Pond
9	Kitchen	19	Loggia
10	Staff Quarters	20	Guest Suite

THE GUEST PAVILION — GROUND FLOOR PLAN

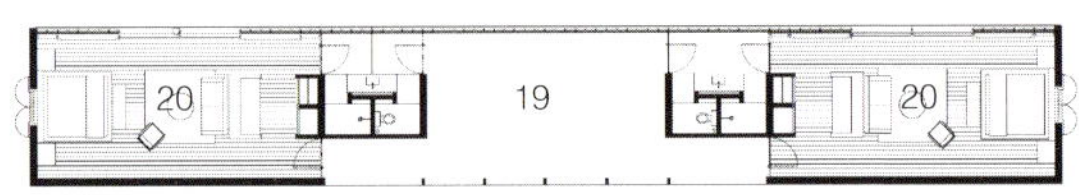

0 1M 5M 10M

Green House

Eagles Ridge, Digana

Architect Madhura Prematilleke
Team Architrave

Located at Eagles Ridge within the Victoria Golf and Country Resort at Digana and accessed via Kandy, the Green House is owned by an English businessman who is an avid golfer. As he travels extensively in Asia in the course of his work, he wished to build a vacation home that, in time, will become his retirement residence. For now, it serves as a wonderful venue to entertain his extended family and business acquaintances invited to play on the golf course, considered by many to be the finest in Sri Lanka. The owner has named the house 'Haritha', which means 'Green' in Sinhala.

The architect of the house, which is built on a precipitous slope that steps down six levels from the entrance and looks southwest through a spectacular wooded valley to the Victoria reservoir and mountain range beyond, is Madhura Prematilleke (57). Prematilleke graduated as an architect from the University of Moratuwa in 1981 and worked for one year with Balkrishna V Doshi and the Vastu Shilpa Foundation in Ahmedabad before embarking on a Master's degree in Urban Design in Finland in 1986. He returned to Sri Lanka in 1991 and leads the designer practice known as Team Architrave. Representing a generation driven by a strong social conscience, he is passionately devoted to producing a modern, eco-conscious Sri Lankan architecture.

Influenced by both Doshi and Finnish late-modernism, Prematilleke taught in the Department of Architecture at the University of Moratuwa for 14 years. He has criticised the so-called 'umbrella aesthetic' that, he says, "carries with it an idealization of rural, usually feudal life. It is an ideology that generates architectural models with an inherent anti-urban bias."[1] Prematilleke has also criticised "the widespread practice, in the name of 'recycling', of scavenging and destroying valuable old buildings and even entire streets so that we may lean on the glory of stolen columns."[2]

The Green House unquestionably employs a modern architectural language. A series of southwest facing glazed cubes, superimposed one upon another, tumbles down the slope, unified by a strong structural concept. The vertical circulation adroitly shifts from the west side of the house to the east side as one descends. The

Previous page left: The house negotiates a steep incline from the entrance level down to the floor of a valley.
Previous page right: Glass façades are shaded by mature trees that were carefully protected during the construction of the house.
Left: The house entrance is one level below the access road.
Opposite top and bottom left: Within the dining area and living areas there is a strong sense of living in the canopy of the surrounding trees.
Opposite bottom right: A strong orthogonal structural grid unifies the architectural composition.

house has an east-facing mono pitch roof and a square water tower. Local regulations played a part in the form, as the house was required to stay within a prescribed angle, set backs of 25m from the boundary were stipulated, and a sloping roof over most of the house was a further requirement.

"At the outset," states Prematilleke, "I observed that the special building rules at the Golf Links were generating buildings which are visually heavy and have large footprints (as a way to fit in their programme within height-restrictive rules). I wished the opposite: that whatever we build must sit lightly upon the ground. Therefore our key focus was on reducing the footprint while at the same time working within the imposed height restrictions. You see the outcome in two aspects: the slim tall sectional form, and the submerged building — so much that, as you arrive, you see nothing of the many levels below."

The house is entered at the highest level via a gate alongside a parking space for two cars. Immediately one descends by two half-flights of stairs, past a lotus pond, to the entrance on the west flank of the house and thence to the master bedroom suite and beyond to a very private roof terrace and an outdoor Jacuzzi. One floor below, there are two more bedrooms and, descending again, one arrives at a stunning two-storey-high living space with a dining area and kitchen. Sliding glass doors give access to a spacious outdoor balcony facing south. A circular iron staircase provides a direct connection from the balcony to the master bedroom two floors above.

At this level, the vertical circulation shifts to the east side of the house, descending to three guest bedrooms and finally to ground level and a gymnasium tucked beneath the house at the lowest level and entered from the garden. For swimming or tennis, guests relocate to the golf clubhouse and mountain bikes are stored beneath the stairs for this purpose.

Completed in 2010, the house is, in essence, a tree house: clear-glazed living spaces and master bedroom all look directly into the surrounding *mara* rain trees and there is a sense of living within the canopy — indeed

the relationship to the trees is vitally important because they provide shade to the south- and west-facing walls. The slender plan is one room wide, so the dwelling has the benefit of natural ventilation, and there are cleverly designed vertical pivoted opening vents alongside each of the large windows for this purpose. By opening these vents air movement can be induced by the *Venturi* effect without opening the sliding doors. Extensive horizontal louvres and pergolas on the west side of the house combat solar gain.

Viewed from the valley, the house is transparent. "Basically it's a concrete inner shell, where all other elements added on are steel, glass and timber," says Prematilleke. "The idea was to design a tropical glass pavilion, which may sound like a contradiction in terms, but this is a concept I have experimented with in several projects, and the house for Mark Green is perhaps its strongest expression. The house uses extensive glazing to benefit from the sweeping views, but is screened effectively by a canopy of trees plus screens and pergolas. A key design decision was to site the house very close to several existing trees, which shelter the glazing and frame the views."

Madhura Prematilleke reveals a masterly control of a large country house programme on a steeply sloping site in a spectacular context and the house has a quality of robustness that has long been a central part of the architect's ethos. In addition, it permits the owner to impose his own style, something that the architect mentioned to me more than a decade ago when he observed that "houses must be able to withstand the personal imprint of the client and not be subdued by the architect's ego".[3]

Prematilleke has progressively developed a type of manifesto that he seeks to adopt in all his projects. It reads:

- Build less — slim the program.
- Build ON less — reduce the footprint, grow trees.
- Build in and out — dissolve barriers between inside and outside.

- Build slender — reduce mass, get slim, make natural light and ventilation possible.
- Build robust — let go to ruin gracefully, reduce the need for maintenance.
- Build light — lightweight structures, layers and skin: touch the earth lightly.
- Build on what is left over — adapt the existing, bring history to life.
- Build ordinary — seek out the beautiful in the everyday, regular is the new special.
- Build safe, not sterile — kill hazard, don't kill joy.
- Build local — feed off local material, local skills.
- Build interim — affordable now, grow later.
- Build hope, not ambition — architecture should offer hope to grow, not be heavy with ambition.
- Build need, not greed — necessity is cool, excess sucks.

[1] Prematilleke, Madhura, 'Beyond the Umbrella and other Stories," Annual Session of the Sri Lanka Institute of Architects, February 1997.
[2] Ibid.
[3] Powell, Robert, 'Robust Architecture', in *The New Asian House*, Select Publishing, Singapore, 2001, p146.

Opposite: The double height living space opens to a wide outdoor balcony with views through trees to the mountains on the horizon and Victoria Lake in the foreground.
Above left: A circular steel staircase ascends from the living room balcony to the roof terrace and master bedroom suite.
Above right: A tranquil lily pond flanks the house entrance.

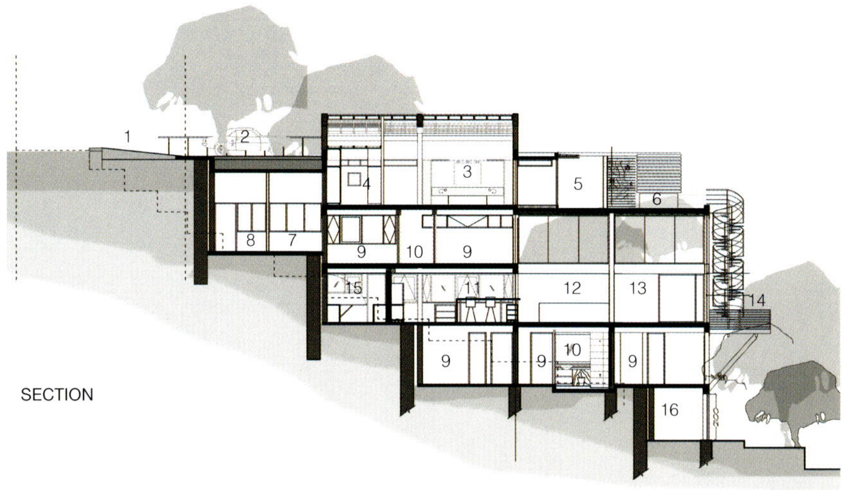

SECTION

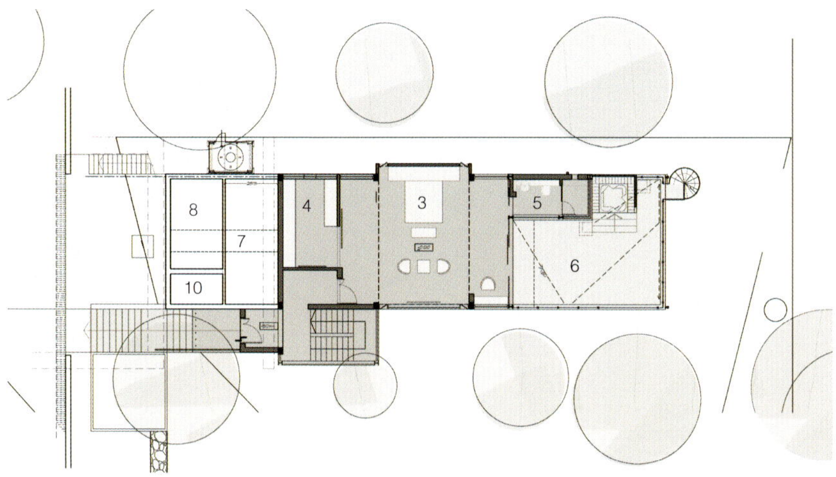

UPPER LEVEL

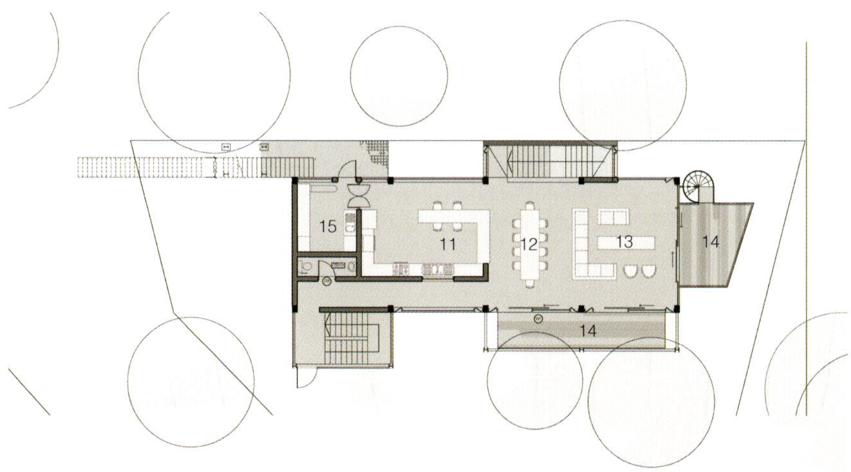

MID LEVEL

1	Entrance	9	Bedroom
2	Car Park	10	Toilet
3	Master Bedroom	11	Kitchen / Pantry
4	Dressing Room	12	Dining
5	Master Bathroom	13	Living
6	Terrace	14	Deck
7	Staff Bedroom	15	Store / Laundry
8	Utility	16	Gym

Opposite top and bottom: The dramatic fall on the site is evident when viewed from a lower bedroom.
Left: The five storey southwest-facing elevation has a quality of robustness that is a hallmark of the architect's work.

Siva and Vasuki House

Digana

Architect **Shayan Kumaradas**

The Siva and Vasuki House is a particularly sensitive response to an exceptional site at Digana, high in the hill country and close to the Victoria Reservoir. A businessman and his wife, a consultant paediatrician, are the owners. Though minimalistic and modern, there are numerous aspects of Tamil culture and the traditional Tamil house embedded in the design: these include an auspiciously placed prayer room with lowered lintel that forces one to lower one's head when approaching the deity, the living room entrance door sourced from Chettinad in Southern India, the traditional *thinnai* (a flat sitting platform) outside the entrance to the living room and a large black carved figure of Ganesha in a garden court.

The owner, Siva Kumaren, was for many years a senior executive of Unilever and is now an importer of bread-making equipment for bakers and commercial kitchens. He and his wife spend part of the year in Ontario, Canada, where they both have residency and part of the year in Colombo with weekends at their Digana home.

The architect of the house is Shayan Kumaradas (42). He hails from Jaffna, where for generations his family has been the custodian of the Nallur Kandaswamy Kovil[1] in Jaffna. As son of the present custodian, he will one day assume the role of sole custodian and administrator in turn. It is a role that has been handed down from father to son for generations. Shayan grew up in the temple environment, surviving the early stages of the ethnic war as the temple became a sanctuary for people fleeing the fighting and was occasionally caught in the cross fire between the LTTE and Government forces. In 1993 he made his way to Colombo to study architecture at the Department of Architecture at the University of Moratuwa and for the next seven years returned home just once a year for the annual festivals. His tutors at Moratuwa included Madhura Prematilleke and Vijitha Basnayaka and he graduated in 1998.

After the Indian peacekeeping force moved into Jaffna in 1987 Siva Kumaren moved to Colombo and when Shayan Kumaradas arrived he acted as a 'big

brother' and became his patron. Kumaradas is the distant cousin of C Anjalendran and he worked with his renowned relative for four years from 2002 before he set up his own practice. He taught for five years at the City School of Architecture and arranged joint programmes with the National University of Singapore and the University of Wisconsin, USA. He talks with passion about all the architects' works he has visited including Rem Koolhaas and Renzo Piano. "Kerry Hill's work is a breath of fresh air," he enthuses.

The house has been six years in the making and the brief is constantly expanding. The intention from the outset was that nothing should be visible of the house on the hillside from the road. It has a high stone wall, a garage door and an inconspicuous entrance from the road at the base of the hill. An austere lobby precedes a long gradual climb via an external stone staircase to the house itself. There are two platforms en route to rest and even to sit down in the shade of a tree by a water lily pond. One eventually arrives at a broad, covered, concrete deck and ahead is the impressive entrance to the living area with the *thinnai* alongside.

The two-storey house has a cleverly 'cranked' plan that ensures maximum views to the Knuckles, the mountain range to the northeast, and Victoria Lake. At dawn the hills are wreathed in mist. It is a simple architecture of stepped levels, horizontal slabs and stone walls of sturdy construction. There are a variety of terraces, inside/outside spaces and cool shaded places with cross ventilation for sitting. There is no air conditioning, but the house is perfectly cool in its absence. The open-sided deck, the cranked plan and the magnificent views to distant hills and the water body remind one of the Kandalama Hotel designed by Geoffrey Bawa that is similarly 'bent' to follow the topography.

Creating the home has been a long process. The owner came to view another site nearby when a villager collecting firewood serendipitously suggested

he look at this site. In the first two years only the garage was completed and in year three the driver's quarters, and then, as and when money became available, the owner gradually built up the stone walls and terraces. Kumaradas shows a keen appreciation of the topography and the entrance sequence is cleverly orchestrated as it ascends from east to west.

"As a weekend or holiday destination," the architect explains, "the Siva and Vasuki House differs from the normal home in this category for it is not in a 'prime location' and the site did not have any obvious views. In fact the architecture 'goes in search of the views' gradually ascending until, at the top of the hill, all becomes apparent and the cranked plan provides a variety of surprises."

A second entrance has been added via a steep vehicular ramp to the south of the house leading to a vehicle court and thence via a shallow pedestrian ramp for the elderly. It is a reminder of the ramps and choreography of spaces at Chitradurga Fort, a citadel in the Vijayanagara Kingdom, the last Hindu Empire of India. There are plans to add a bathing pool in the lower garden court and a substantial part of the remaining site has been utilized as a pepper plantation.

Put simply, the design is an architectural response to the site and the owner's desire for privacy, but it has

Previous page left and right: The house sits atop a hill. Its cranked plan provides dramatic views of the Knuckles mountain range and Victoria Lake.

Opposite and top right: There are a variety of open and shaded cool terraces with cross ventilation for sitting and contemplation.

Above left: A view from the upper terrace to the lower entrance.

Above: The garden court with a line of oil lamps that leads to the carved figure of Ganesha.

a self-sufficient fortress-like quality as well. The house was intentionally cut off with no name, no number and no identification, for the owners sought solitude for communion with God and with nature. Yet its robust external appearance contrasts with its beautiful sensitive details. The bathroom details and door details are of exceptional quality. South Indian classical music plays continuously and a love seat in the living room adds a romantic note. Architect and client are very close friends and the house was, in part, built as a place to share weekends together with the architect's young children. "It is a house created by love," the owner concludes.

The rituals of lighting oil lamps around Ganesha and the wall lamps leading from a wood carving of Nagaraja the Snake King add to the aura of the house. Kumaradas tells an intriguing anecdote of a snake, an albino cobra that lived on the site and now keeps watch over the property.

[1] Nallur Kovil is one of the most significant Hindu temples in the country, situated in Jaffna District of the Northern Province. The presiding deity is Lord Murugan in the form of the holy Vel. The present temple was built in 1734 by Shayan Kumaradas's ancestor, Ragunatha Maappana Mudaliyar, during the Dutch rule and occupation of the Jaffna Peninsula.

Opposite top left: A traditional *thinnai* or flat platform provides a place for greeting guests outside the entrance to the living room. **Opposite top right:** The house is approached from below via a series of external stone stairs with intermediate platforms. **Opposite bottom left:** A quiet place for contemplation at the upper verandah. **Opposite bottom right:** The focus of the upper garden court is a large black figure of Ganesha. **Left:** The carved living room entrance door was sourced from Chettinad in Southern India. The artwork is 'Sunburst', a batik by Ena de Silva.

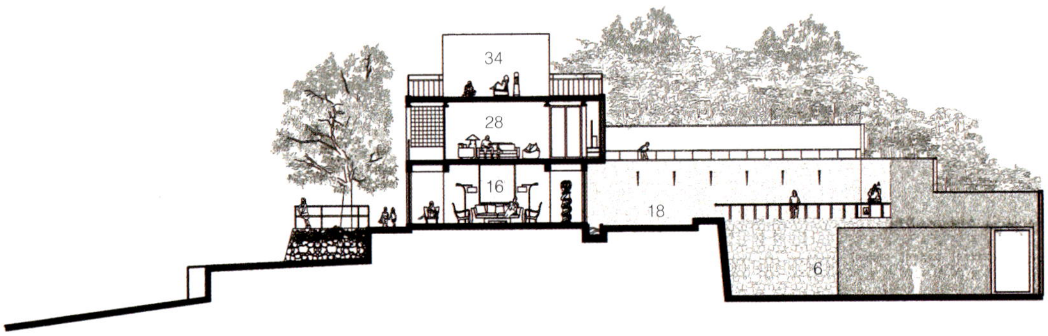

SECTION

1 Entrance
2 Carport
3 Service Entrance
4 'Siyambala' Terrace
5 'Manel' Pond
6 Pool (Future) Terrace
7 Pepper Cultivation
8 Room 1
9 Kitchenette
10 Toilet 1
11 Caretaker's Quarters
12 Room 2
13 Toilet 2
14 Entrance Verandah
15 Shrine Room
16 Living
17 Dining
18 Dining Terrace
19 Kitchen
20 Store 1
21 Store 2
22 Service Court
23 Staff Toilet
24 Upper Level Car Park
25 Bedroom 3
26 Toilet 3
27 Verandah
28 Family Living
29 Bedroom 4
30 Toilet 4
31 Bedroom 5
32 Toilet 5
33 Terrace
34 Roof Terrace

Opposite: A wood carving of Nagaraja, the Snake King, graces the dining area. **Right:** The Hindu lion carvings are from an old chariot in India.

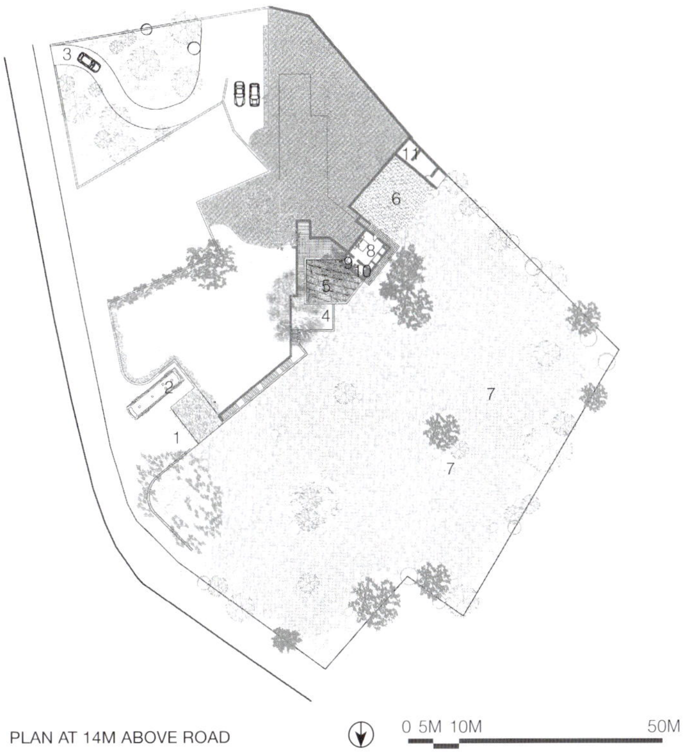

PLAN AT 14M ABOVE ROAD

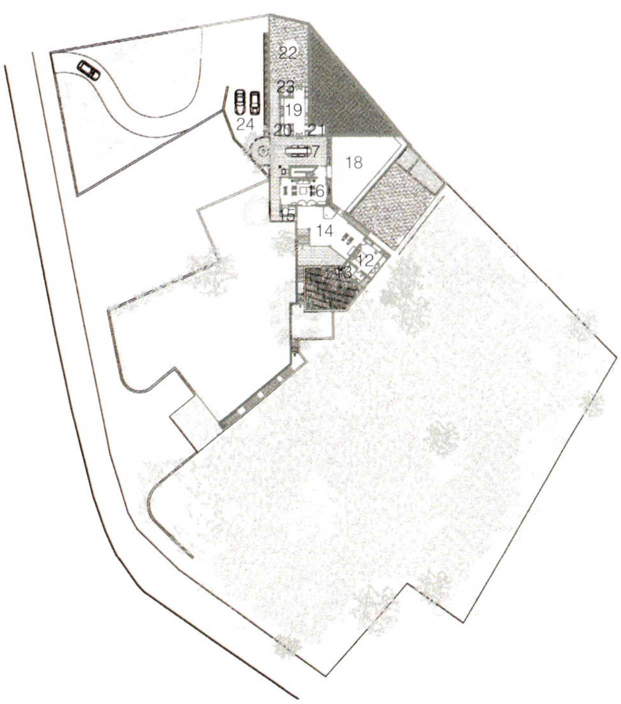

PLAN AT 17M ABOVE ROAD

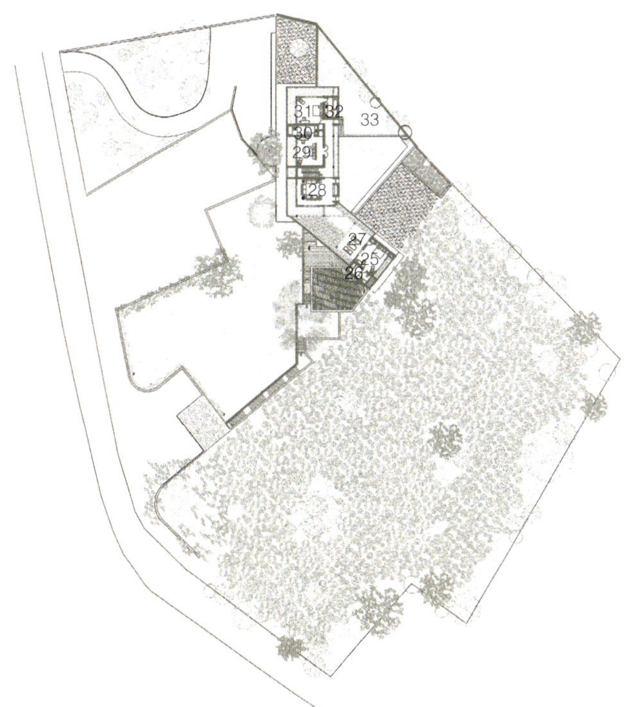

PLAN AT 20M ABOVE ROAD

Above: The main house is a two-storey barn-like building.
Right: The outdoor dining area beneath a sheltering tamarind tree.
Opposite: A processional route ascends from the car park via a series of shallow platforms to a 'gateway' in the forest.

Madanayake Retreat

Ridigama

Architect Ragi Kadirgamar

The Madanayake Retreat at Ridigama is the vacation home of a Sri Lankan businessman, his Australian wife and their children. The site is within a former rubber estate, but there is little evidence of the earlier use other than the ruins of the estate manager's bungalow. The owner of the house lived in Sydney for 20 years but returned in 1995 to manage the family firm, the Ceylon Pencil Company. He married his Australian bride on a rocky outcrop at the northeast corner of the Ridigama site in 2009. They were entranced by the silence of the site and now visit with family and friends whenever possible.

The architect of the dwelling is Ragi Kadirgamar (47). For four years, from 2004 to 2007 he lived in the same Colombo apartment block as the owners and was best man at their wedding. Kadirgamar was propelled on his architectural career by his aunt who introduced him to Geoffrey Bawa. He worked in the office of Colombo architects Kahawita de Silva Associates for six months after school, and then studied for six years at the University of Brighton School of Architecture in the UK where he developed an interest in ecological architecture. When he qualified in 1994 he was offered a place in Geoffrey Bawa's office, but decided to seek experience further afield and was employed for a short period in the office of William Lim Architects in Singapore.

The Madanayake Retreat is approached via a road that passes the 2nd-century Ridi Vihara (Silver) Buddhist temple. Built on a rocky outcrop, the entrance is a processional route, ascending via a number of shallow platforms from a car park in a clearing. It is an enchanting sequence that builds up anticipation until the gable of the house is glimpsed through the trees. The site is dry in February but when the rains come in April small ponds form on the rocky outcrop and lotus flowers appear as if by magic. In October it is very cool and a wonderful playground for a young family.

The main house is a huge two-storey barn-like building with a shallow pitched tiled roof raised on concrete *piloti*. The ground floor is given over to a tall open-sided living space and a lower dining space. The master bedroom is located above the dining space.

Left: The house looks west across a flat grassy area to a lap pool at the very edge of the plateau. From the pool there are views of the distant hills. **Opposite:** The living/dining room and the bedrooms enclose a sandy courtyard shaded by mature trees.

To the east of the main house are three stone and glass sleeping pavilions with mono pitch roofs. The main house, two of the pavilions and a single-storey kitchen block enclose a sandy courtyard.

The whole ensemble has a curious ambience not unlike a small outback 'station' in Australia, a sort of 'shearing shed' surrounded by sleeping quarters. There is a shaded outdoor sitting place beneath a large tamarind tree and, from a look out point on a rocky promontory, there are distant views of hills to the west and southwest. The imagery is perhaps appropriate for the owners. The orthogonal layout also appears to take as a precedence, Lunuganga, the highly influential garden designed by Geoffrey Bawa at Bentota. Kadirgamar confirms this to be the case, saying, "When I returned to Sri Lanka after my postgraduate studies, I spent several weekends with Geoffrey Bawa at Lunuganga, and this did inspire the entrance sequence of Ridigama."

Kadirgamar describes the design process in detail: "The concept was to make the house as eco-friendly as possible within the clients' overall brief. I spent many days and nights observing and experiencing the site and climatic conditions. The final positioning of the house took over a year of regular site visits until it became clear one day that the view to the lake in the distance was the key axis. The sand courtyard space is to contrast the openness of the site, and provides at night in particular a more intimate space that can be lit with candles under the tree canopies. The plan was finalised on site with strings and timber pegs to demarcate the position of the buildings, incorporating the existing trees, rock outcrops, and level changes."

"The pond on the kitchen roof," he contines, "was a change in the original design after a site visit I made and saw the rainwater that had collected on the recently poured reinforced concrete slab, and thought the reflections looked rather beautiful. The house is completely self sufficient because rainwater is stored

Left top: The dining table is a recycled temple cart.
Left, centre and below: The kitchen and bathrooms share a restrained palette of materials including polished cement floors, sliding timber doors and windows, and plaster ceilings.
Opposite: Three temple carts have been adapted for day beds in the living area. A figure of Ganesha overlooks the open-sided room.

in large tanks for the dry months, and filtered using sand and carbon filters. Solar panels supply hot water. Much of the stone was salvaged from the old plantation house on the site. The timber columns are five-year-old teak trees, felled and treated on the property. Materials were sourced locally where possible to reduce the carbon footprint. The stone steps on the processional entrance are salvaged from a floor of a Hindu temple demolished in Colombo. The balconies are made from recycled railway sleepers and the colour of the columns in the barn-like structure were selected to blend with the grey of the tree trunks. The green colour cement tile roof was chosen to blend with the site's vegetation, and to withstand the stampeding monkeys."

The owner of the house collects religious works of art and, intriguingly for a Singhalese household, there are a number of Hindu artifacts in the living space beneath the high roof including an image of Ganesha and several giant wooden wheels formerly used for temple carts that have been fashioned into day beds.

In the tall pavilion there is a sense of living at the interface of the built world and the natural world. It is a marvelous place for dinner, surrounded by the sound of the forest at night and cooled by a gentle breeze. Ceiling fans supplement the cross ventilation. The sleeping pavilions are not as successful in dealing with the climate as, by necessity, they have to be enclosed to prevent wildlife and vermin entering. Although correctly orientated away from the sun at its zenith and with east-facing stone walls, they nevertheless become stuffy. External timber louvres on the west façade might mitigate this problem and obviate the need for bamboo 'tats' within the bedrooms. By contrast, there are delightful open-to-sky bathrooms in all three sleeping pavilions.

The proximity to nature goes further as an exuberant colony of monkeys contest possession of the site emerging at dusk and leaping around noisily on the roof.

Left: The approach to the house is via a series of terraces and steps, a feature the architect attributes to the influence of Geoffrey Bawa's garden at Lunuganga.

SECTION

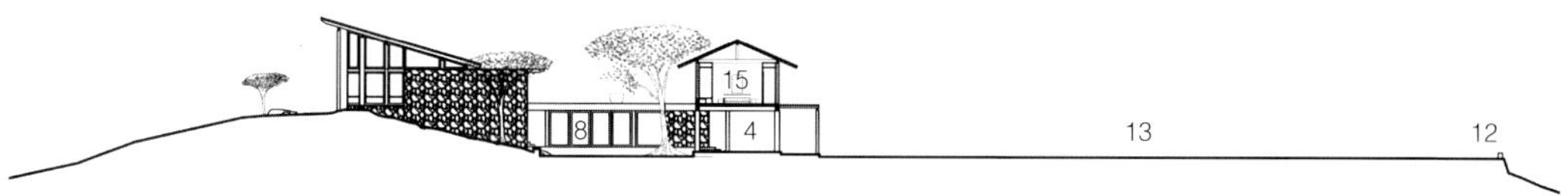

1 Driveway
2 Entry Pavilion
3 Terrace
4 Living
5 Dining
6 Kitchen
7 Kitchen Store
8 Courtyard
9 Bathroom / WC
10 Store
11 Swimming Pool
12 Terrace
13 Lawn
14 Sitting Area
15 Master Bedroom
16 Master Bath / WC
17 Roof Pond
18 Bedroom
19 Balcony
20 Pond
21 Bathroom / WC
22 Courtyard

GROUND FLOOR PLAN

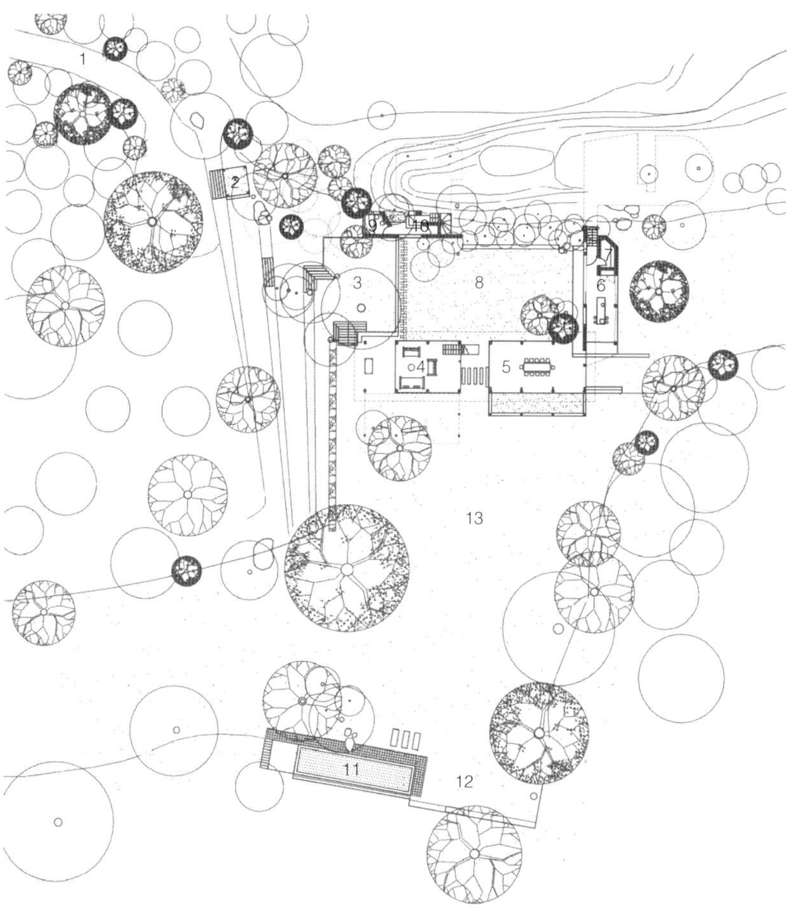

FIRST FLOOR PLAN

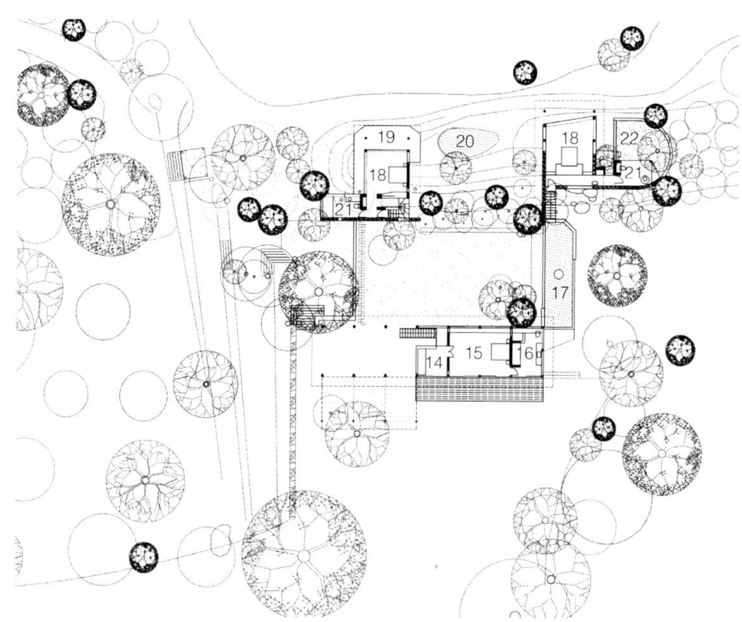

Maddumage House

Madawala Ulpotha, Matale

Architect **Thisara Thanapathy**
Thisara Thanapathy Architects

The Maddumage House is the idyllic weekend retreat of a former stockbroker and his family. The house has a cruciform plan of Miesien simplicity consisting of two key elements: a 40-metre-long x four-metre-wide horizontal timber walkway and a minimalist two-storey structure of steel and glass with permanent timber louvres on the east and west elevations that spans over the walkway. Located approximately three hours drive northeast of Colombo, the house is constructed largely with salvaged materials — timber and steel were transported to the site from a demolished factory in Colombo and the walkway is made of recycled railway sleepers. Local labour was used for the construction.

The architect of the house is Thisara Thanapathy (50), a 1992 graduate of the Department of Architecture at the University of Moratuwa. After working with Ashley de Vos and Design Group 5 he established his own practice in 1999.

Arriving at the house, vehicles are parked at the base of a hill to the north and the final 100 metres is a gentle climb on foot. Around the house the owner has planted more than 12 hectares (30 acres) of teak trees that are being farmed commercially. The entrance to the house is at first elusive and then, quite suddenly, it is apparent. The timber walkway stretches to the east, flanked on the south side by a two-metre-high concrete wall. There is a tiny Buddhist shrine to the north of the entrance.

Looking along the walkway, it is seen to penetrate through the house and terminate some way beyond with a viewing platform embedded in the teak plantation. The rough texture of the railway sleepers slows progress and allows the house to be gradually revealed and appreciated. In sharp contrast, the building is a delicate, albeit robust, structure raised on I-section steel *piloti*. The dining room to the south of the walkway has frameless glass sliding doors, while the floors are made from smooth-planed railway sleepers. The kitchen and storage are within a small solid core. To the north of

the walkway is a minimal circular steel staircase that ascends to the main living spaces comprising two bedrooms with ensuite bathrooms and a sitting room, the latter located above the walkway and with views east and west. Glass is not used on the upper floor except for in shower cubicles. Bedrooms are further protected by external tats and the zinc coated-steel roof has a pitch of 5 degrees with wide eaves. The contrast between the two main elements in the plan form is acute.

The eastern end of the walkway, which is elevated about six metres above the terrain, is a sublime place to sit, to enjoy the sound of silence, to view the rising sun and the Knuckles mountain range or to dine al fresco in the evening. The house, to use a phrase borrowed from the Australian architect Glenn Murcutt, 'touches the ground lightly'.

The Maddumage House is a brilliant example of the fusion of traditional responses to climate with a modern architectural form. One of the first 'rules' of building in the tropics (often ignored or forgotten) is that the solar mitigation measures should be outside the glass, particularly on the east and west elevations, and that glass, when used, should be shaded. Placing blinds inside a room does nothing to reduce solar heat gain. Another 'rule' is that houses should wherever possible be elevated to permit wind to ventilate beneath the lower floor and minimise the damage to the ecology. Yet another is that houses should be 'one room wide' to permit cross ventilation, passive air-cooling and natural light. All of this is understood by Thanapathy. As a result, the Maddumage House has a very low carbon footprint and no fixed fans or air-conditioning.

Thanapathy is clear where his practice is heading, saying, "From the inception of our practice, we focused on the aesthetic experience of spatial form, delivering sensual delight to our clients while addressing their

practical requirements. Over the years, we have come to emphasize equally caring for both body and mind through design: relaxation, nourishment and rejuvenation. We treat the spaces we create as sanctuaries from the stresses of modern society, antidotes to relentless consumerism and environmental destruction. As such, our designs advance ecologically sensible solutions, involving innovative technologies and architectural forms."

Thisara Thanapathy is one of the leading architects of his generation and received a commendation for the design of the Maddumage House in the 2010/2011 Geoffrey Bawa Awards. Coincidentally, the timber and steel used in the construction of the house were recycled from a factory building in Colombo designed by Bawa's former practice Edwards, Reid & Begg and demolished in 2008.

Previous page left: The house section is designed so that the roof and louvre-clad upper floor protect the lower floor from solar gain.
Previous page right: A 40-metre-long timber walkway fashioned from recycled railway sleepers unifies the plan.
Opposite: A view along the timber walkway from the sitting area/viewing platform at the southern end.
Above left: The opposite view from the northern entrance.
Above right: The bedrooms cantilever into the canopy of the surrounding teak plantation.

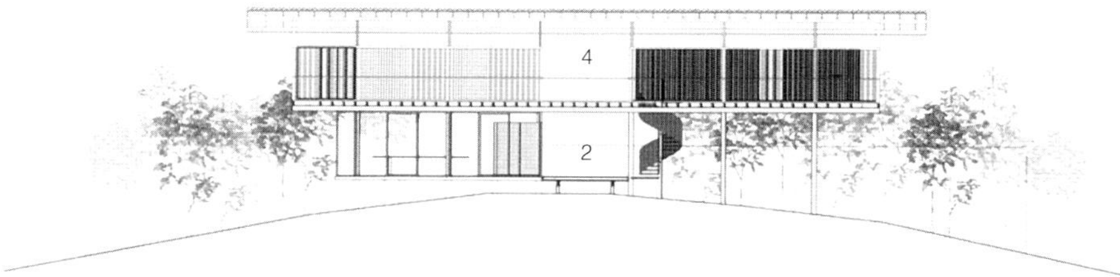

Opposite top: The kitchen and breakfast area projects into the plantation. The roof and overhanging upper floor shade the glass walls.
Opposite bottom left and right: With the exception of the ensuite bathrooms, glass is eschewed on the upper floor that comprises two bedrooms.

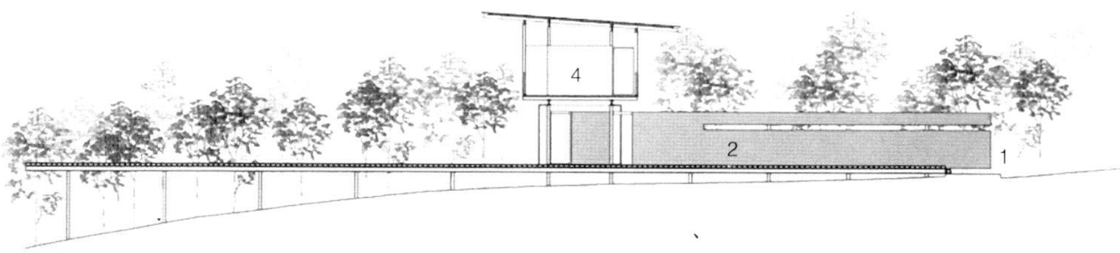

SECTION

1	Approach	5	Bedroom
2	Viewing Deck / Living / Dining	6	Toilet
3	Pantry Dining	7	Wardrobe
4	Sitting Area	8	Storage & Refrigerator

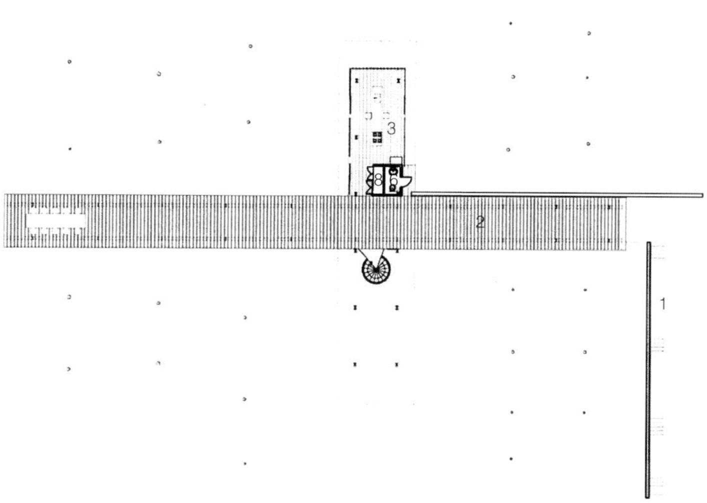

GROUND FLOOR PLAN

0 1M 5M 10M

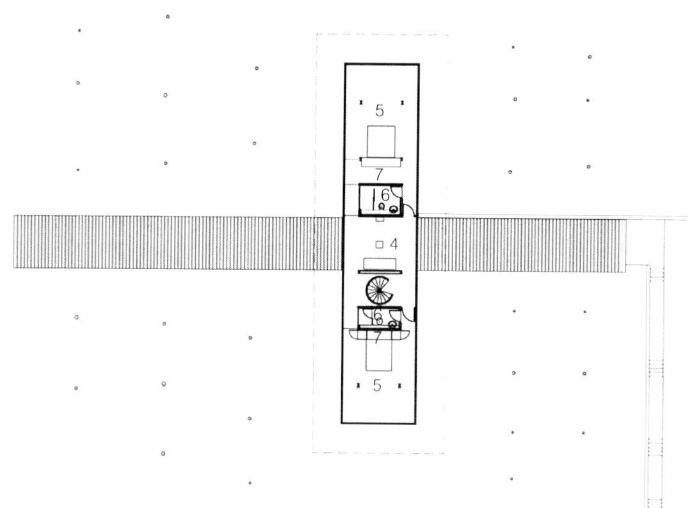

FIRST FLOOR PLAN

Right: The path to the house ascends via a series of shallow platforms from the parking space. A view of the ocean is delayed until one reaches a bridge at the upper level.
Opposite: The house viewed from the parking space on the lower slopes.
Overleaf left: The ocean is dramatically revealed beyond the infinity pool and pool deck.
Overleaf right: A bridge, flanked by a bar counter, connects the master bedroom to the pavilion.

Kadju House

Tangalla

Architect Pradeep Kodikara

The Kadju House is a captivating holiday villa at Tangalla on the southern coast of Sri Lanka. It takes its name from its location on the site of a cashew grove (*kadju* translates as "cashew"). The owner is a Bangalore-based anthropologist, ecologist and writer who came to work in Sri Lanka in 2003.

The approach to the house is finely orchestrated: turning south off the Tangalla Road a narrow unmade track climbs up a gentle rise, then, cresting the summit, it descends past the western flank of the house and plunges into an area of mature trees. A view of the ocean is tantalisingly withheld. Leaving the car park below the house one must then ascend on foot via a series of platforms and shallow steps to a wide lobby that doubles as the dining area. Finally, after ascending a dogleg stair to the terrace that bridges the lobby, a stunning panoramic view of the Indian Ocean is revealed beyond an infinity lap pool. It is a magical sequence that serves as an introduction to the pleasures of the house.

The plan is an 'L'-shaped configuration with the longer (western) leg thrusting south. The house has four bedrooms, two to the west of the central dining space and two to the east. Three bedrooms have open-to-sky bathrooms, each with a distinctive configuration. Three of the bedrooms also enjoy south-facing sun decks and the house steps down the slope so that the pool deck is above the service area and the lower bedroom, while the master bedroom and the sitting area are at the upper level with views south to the horizon. Each of the four bedrooms enjoys a degree of autonomy. Overall there is a wonderful openness to the house and days are passed at the interface of the built and natural environment — the very essence of a house in the tropics. Dinner under the stars is a magical experience with a cool breeze off the ocean.

A fifth guest bedroom is located in the Cinnamon Tower, a three-storey watchtower-like structure with a steep external stair located to the north of the main house. The tower also houses a ground floor Ayurvedic spa and a rooftop water tank and it is clad in cinnamon sticks.

The architect of the house is Pradeep Kodikara (45) who studied at the City School of Architecture in Colombo from 1991 to 1997. He recalls his time at

WOOLF IN CEYLON

CSA with affection for his first-year design tutor was C Anjalendran; in his second year he was tutored by Anura Ratnavibhushana and in his third year he had Turner Wickramasinghe as his mentor — all widely respected names in the architectural profession. Kodikara worked for C Anjalendran from 1991 to 1992 and with Geoffrey Bawa from 1994 to 1995 on additions to the Sindbad Garden Hotel in Kalutara and a hotel project in Ahungalla. He set up his own practice in 1997.

The Kadju House was completed in 2007. Originally designed as a writer's retreat, it was featured in *Condé Nast Traveller* (UK)[1] and has become much in demand as a holiday villa. A gentle meandering path leads down from the house to a deserted white sandy beach in Seenimodara Bay.

Interior décor takes its inspiration from the colours of the cashew tree. While most finishes are off-form concrete, polished cement, timber and lime-washed plaster, some walls and soft furnishings are highlighted in the deep red shade of the cashew apple.

In conversation Kodikara reels off a list of Sri Lankan architects he admires and who in one way or another have influenced his architecture, including Geoffrey Bawa, Minnette de Silva, Valentine Gunasekara and C Anjalendran. Some clues to his architectural inclination can also be gleaned from a list of international practitioners he admires including Charles Eames, John Pawson, Alvaro Siza, Renzo Piano, Glenn Murcutt, Studio Gang, Tadao Ando and Peter Zumthor.

"I let issues at hand influence my design approach," explains Kodikara. "My widely different style is shaped by place, time, the client, and of course the budget. I strive to incorporate environmentally appropriate design in a manner that eventually renders it a distinct part of the architecture itself. If there is any one element that unites all my work it is the constant reference to the outside world, which for me is paramount and I think, essential in tropical architecture."

[1] "25 Best Beach Villas in the World," *Condé Nast Traveller* (UK), February 2010.

Above: A tall bedroom with open-to-sky ensuite bathroom is orientated towards the ocean. A feature-wall is clad in cinnamon.
Right and far right: The three-storey Cinnamon Tower houses an Ayurvedic spa, a guest bedroom and a water tank.
Opposite: A south-facing bedroom opens to an external patio.

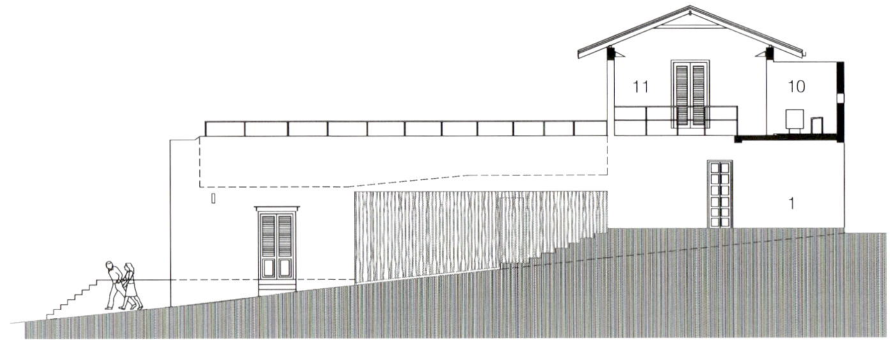

SECTION

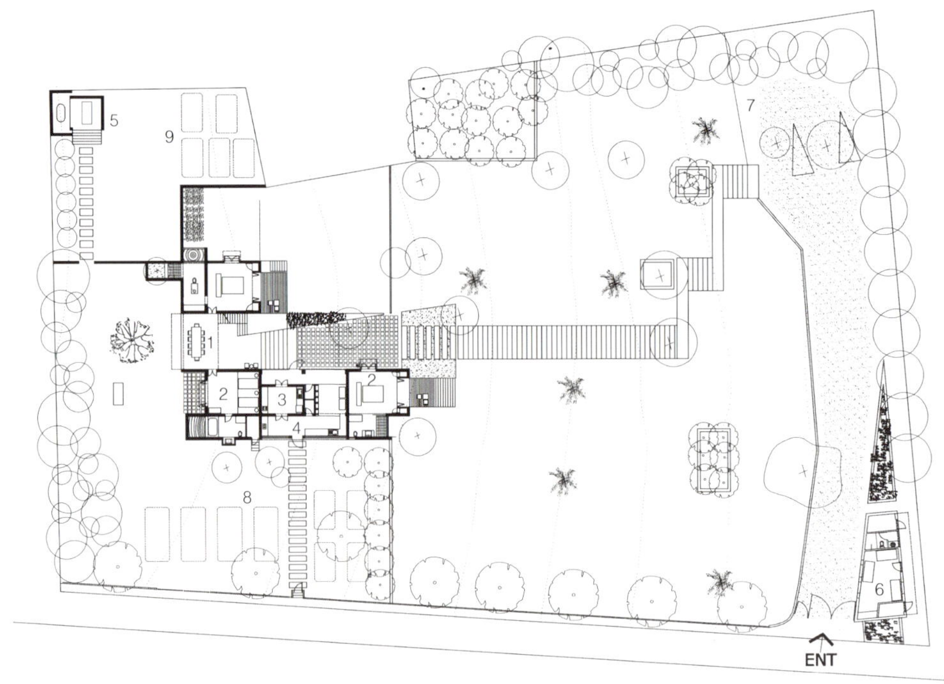

SITE PLAN

0 1M 5M 10M

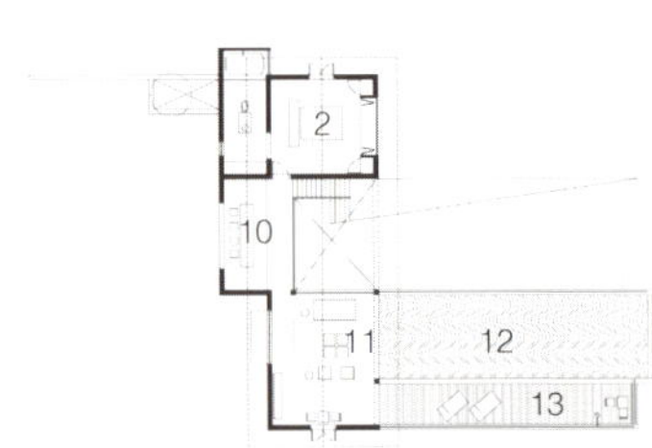

1	Foyer / Dining	8	Fruit Garden
2	Bedroom	9	Herb Garden
3	Pantry	10	Bar
4	Kitchen	11	Pavilion
5	Spa	12	Pool
6	Staff	13	Pool Terrace
7	Parking		

FIRST FLOOR PLAN

Opposite top, centre and bottom: The architect employs a restrained palette of materials – off form concrete, polished cement, timber and lime-washed plaster with splashes of colour on walls and soft furnishings derived from the deep-red colour of the cashew apple.

Right: The naturally ventilated dining terrace viewed from rising ground to the north. The house received the prestigious 2014 Geoffrey Bawa Award for Architecture.

Villa Vista

Mirissa

Architect Shigeru Ban

Villa Vista is the spectacular coastal residence of Koenraad Pringiers, a Belgian businessman who was raised in Sri Lanka and has lived in the country for many years. To design his home located on high ground overlooking Weligama Bay, he engaged the renowned Japanese architect Shigeru Ban and requested that the house take advantage of the breathtaking views from the three-hectare hilltop location.

Shigeru Ban (57) was born in Tokyo, Japan. He studied at the Tokyo University of the Arts, and then at the Southern California Institute of Architecture (SCI-Arc). Later he went to the Cooper Union in New York, where he studied under John Hejduk and graduated in 1984. In January 2014 he was awarded the prestigious Pritzker Prize for architecture.

The architect initially identified three important viewpoints and has composed the sculptural form of the house to frame these views. The first is a view of the ocean gradually revealed as one ascends to a col on the southern flank of the house. This is captured in a perpendicular frame as the culmination of the axial entrance path. The second view is a dramatic panorama of Weligama Bay from the hilltop, which is enclosed in a horizontal frame from the living area. The third view is of sunset lighting up cliffs to the north west captured in a 'square' timber frame from the master bedroom.

Simultaneously the architect has zoned the house and composed it in section as a series of platforms with stairs negotiating the 1.5 metre difference between each zone. Thus having followed a gradually ascending linear axis from the drop-off point via a series of platforms, a flight of 10 steps leads to the entrance court. A lone frangipani tree occupies the centre of the court. A further flight of 10 risers ascends to the reception area and yet another flight of 10 steps leads to the dining area. Finally one climbs the last flight of 1.5 metres to arrive at the living space and a dramatic panorama of the bay is revealed.

In common with other projects by his office, Ban employs spatial continuity to create a seamless flow between indoor and outdoor spaces. The processional route is in this genre and the final 'explosive' view at the summit of the hill is totally breathtaking.

A triangular 'elbow' links the living room and dining area to the master bedroom and the spacious service area beneath the dining area. Two delightful guest bedrooms are accessed via a steel bridge at the southern end of the living room. The bridge structure forms the uppermost element of the 'frame' that concludes the entrance axis referred to earlier.

Considerable attention was devoted to the design of the large pitched roof. The steel structure spans 22 metres and the roof is covered with a light cement board for waterproofing, then layered with woven coconut leaves intended to prevent the house from overheating. The ceiling above the living/dining room is assembled from teak strips woven into a large wickerwork pattern with a myriad tiny LED lights that sparkle like stars in the evening.

The scale of the 825-sq-m house is monumental, but it simultaneously has tactile qualities that impart a human dimension. There are multiple textures, from the modular external paving blocks, to the riprap stone walling, to the triangular precast blocks that form the courtyard walls, to the teak louvred shutters in the dining area and the cardboard tubes used for the wavy ceiling in the subterranean gym/games room/ audio room. A small blue terrazzo-tiled waterfall descends from the pool at the upper level to the entrance court via the reception area and reflects glittering patterns on the walls. Large artworks adorn the walls of the house, most of them by the owner's mother Saskia Pintelon. Some of the furniture is designed by Shigeru Ban and manufactured by the owner's brother, Jacob Pringiers.

Previous page: The living area has a stunning panoramic view of Weligama Bay. The furniture is designed by Shigeru Ban and manufactured by Jacob Pringiers. The ceiling is woven teak strips.
Opposite: The east-facing landward façade of the house is clad with tall louvred teak screens.
Above, clockwise from left: The approach to the house is via a series of platforms from a drop-off point to the entrance court; there is a seamless flow between indoor and outdoor space. The master bathroom looks out to the ocean. An aerial view of the house reveals it is deeply embedded in the landscape.

Completed in 2010, construction was carried out in association with Philip Weeraratne, the principal of PWA Architects. Of the Villa Vista project he notes, "We worked closely with Shigeru Ban's European office in Paris. My colleague Ravindu 'Ravi' Karunanayake was pivotal during the design and construction process and Yasunori Harano was seconded to the PWA offices throughout the construction period."

Criticism can be leveled at the house on some aspects: for example, the guardhouse that precedes the processional route to the entrance court is understated to the point that it can be bypassed easily when arriving by car with the result that one enters the entrance court by the 'back door'. Thus the arrival sequence may not be fully appreciated. The house has also received some adverse criticism because of its exposure to the southwest monsoon, but it has an exhilarating series of spaces that culminate in the breathtaking view of Weligama Bay from the living room.

The essence of the house is that it gives the owner a place for solitude. An unmade track on the north flank of the house, accessed from the entrance court, leads to a clifftop gazebo and a steep path down to the beach. There is a sense of isolation and quietness. It is a place where the life of the city can be left behind and one can simply enjoy the silence. Alternatively, it could become a place for a lively party where neighbours will not be disturbed or inconvenienced.

Above left: The reception area with stairs ascending to the living area and a soaring bridge to the two guest bedrooms. The large painting entitled 'Weligama Bay 2010' is by Saskia Pintelon.
Above right: The entrance to the reception space with teak louvres.
Opposite: The culmination of the processional route to the entrance court. Ten steps up lead to a gentle waterfall.
Overleaf top left: The formal dining area. Furniture is designed by Shigeru Ban and manufactured by the owner's brother.
Overleaf bottom left: The master bedroom.
Overleaf right: Triangular perforated concrete blocks are employed to create a screen around the entrance court.

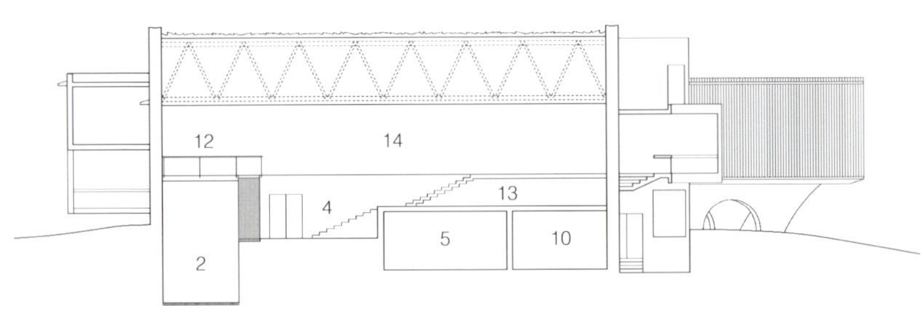

SECTION

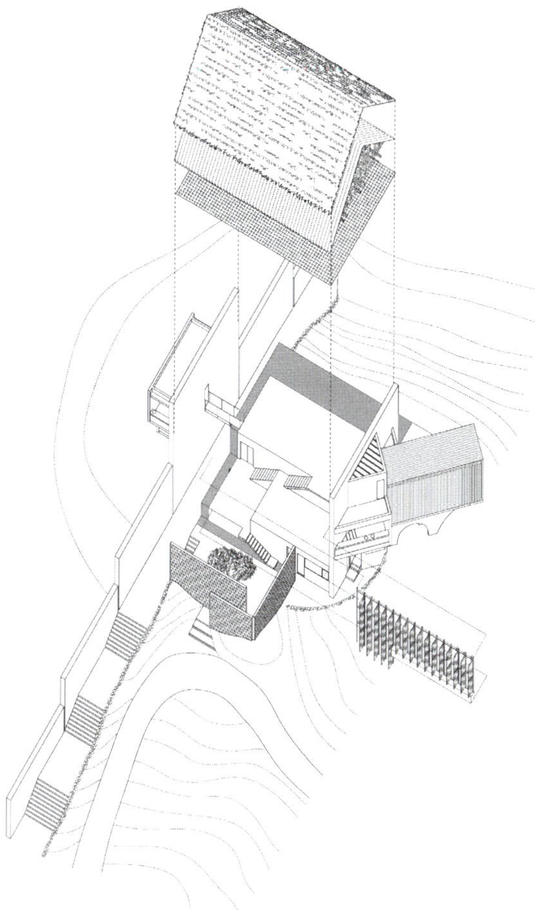

EXPLODED AXON METRIC

1	Pool Base	10	Staff Room
2	Entrance Avenue	11	Staff Bathroom / WC
3	Entry Court	12	Bridge
4	Reception	13	Formal Dining
5	Dining	14	Living
6	Games Room / Audio Visual / Dining	15	Master Bedroom
7	Kitchen	16	Master Closet
8	Guest Room	17	Master Bathroom / WC
9	Guest Bathroom / WC	18	Swimming Pool
		19	Movable Deck

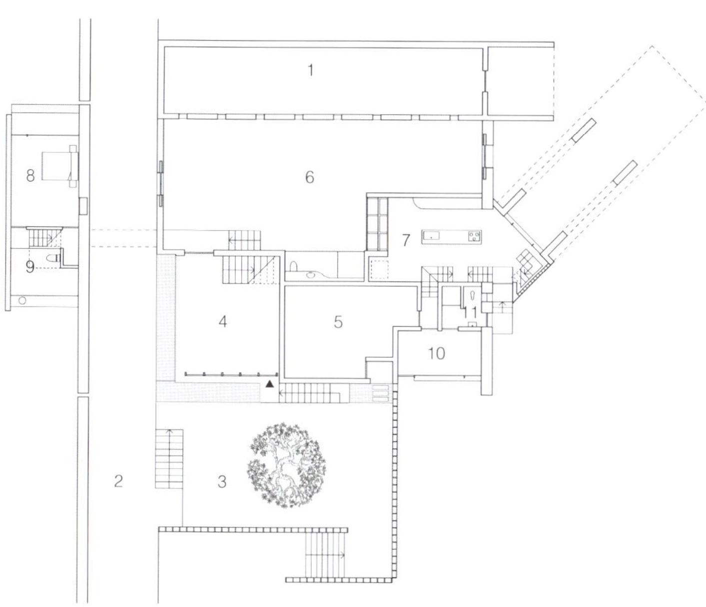

GROUND FLOOR PLAN

0 1M 5M 10M

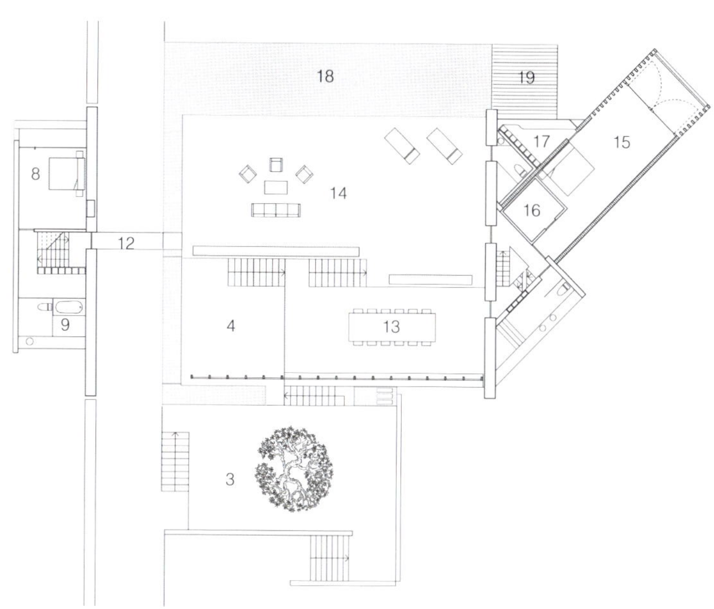

FIRST FLOOR PLAN

Pringiers House

Mirissa

Architect Tadao Ando

Pringiers House is the dramatic clifftop home of Pierre Pringiers, a Belgian industrialist and philanthropist, and his artist wife Saskia Pintelon, who have lived in Sri Lanka for three decades. Perched on the cliffs above Weligama Bay, the house was a present from Pierre to his wife. The *raison d'être* of their residence is the huge studio where Pintelon produces her distinctive and much sought after canvasses. When asked who she wished to design their home she was unequivocal in her choice of the Japanese master Tadao Ando and there followed a short period where his services were entreated before he accepted the commission.

Tadao Ando (72) is one of the most renowned contemporary Japanese architects. He is also one of that extremely rare breed of gifted architects in the world who is self-taught (he was a professional boxer prior to becoming an architect). He has been a visiting professor at Yale, Columbia and Harvard Universities and he has won almost every architectural award imaginable, including the Pritzker Prize in 1995.

The plan of the house is essentially an 'N' shape with two parallel 'wings' orientated approximately north to south. One wing contains the reception, master bedroom suite, and Pierre's study, while the other contains four guest bedrooms with en-suite bathrooms. They are connected by a dynamic diagonal element that includes a 20-metre-long dining/living room beneath an infinity swimming pool projecting to the southwest. The two-storey living/dining room has a ramp down with a sloping ceiling reflecting the form of the pool above. At the push of a button, the huge window at the end of the living room slides smoothly down into a basement void. In addition, projecting at right angles, to the northwest of the entrance, is a tapering, rectangular wing that contains the artist's studio and a gallery. An elevator connects the principle functions in the house.

The positioning of the house has been done cleverly, even though Tadao Ando himself did not visit the site. He relied instead on the project architect Hidehiro Yano who liaised with local architects PWA. Ando worked from maps and ground surveys and photographs and his colleague's first-hand knowledge to distill the

Previous page left: An aerial view of the house reveals the dramatic location overlooking Weligama Bay.
Previous page right: A somewhat austere entrance to the house speaks of exclusion, privacy and the notion of a place to contemplate and escape the hectic pace of life in the city.
Left, top and bottom: The pool deck in the early morning.
Below: A triangular beam of light strikes the wall in the entrance plaza.
Opposite: A shaft of light animates the living space.

essence of the site, the framing of views to the Indian Ocean and the points of interest — the surf in the bay, the red cliffs, Taprobane Island, Crow Island, Snake Island and Parai Duwa — all features captured in one of Pintelon's paintings.[1]

The journey to the house begins at an unmarked black iron gate on the Matara Road and then via a paved road that gradually ascends to the south of the house before circling around to the north and the point of entry. The house is gradually revealed. A triangular entrance courtyard beyond a second security gate funnels one to a grand staircase that sharply diminishes in width as one ascends to arrive on an open deck with a reverse triangle looking out to Weligama Bay.

Initially it is a struggle to comprehend the geometry of the house. Simple from an aerial perspective, once in the building it becomes a labyrinth for exploration with surprises and delight at every turn. Saskia Pintelon's vast two-storey studio with a huge west-facing window has a gallery running around two sides and stairs down from a bridge over the work area. It is a grand space and characteristic of Ando with a huge cruciform west window. But it is the 'connections' that delight — the 'left over' or interstitial spaces between the buildings. Deep light wells penetrate to the basement. There is a constant interplay of darkness and light.

The local Architect of Record on the house was Philip Weeraratne of PWA Architects. Weeraratne knew the Pringiers's son, Koenraad, socially and jokingly offered "to carry Tadao Ando's bag" if he were appointed to design the Pringiers House. He pitched for the job of local architect with just a two-room office. "It was a miracle when we were selected," he says, "I put it down simply to divine intervention."

Building of the house commenced in May 2004 and it was completed in 2007. "Ando planned to come to the site," says Weeraratne, "but it was during the war. Visits were arranged but subsequently cancelled due to some kind of incident or a bomb going off close to the planned visit. I am certain he is proud of the result." Design drawings were done in Osaka and the precision of the off-form concrete is impressive. Philip Weeraratne

Above: The artist's studio – a quiet creative space. The window with cruciform fenestration is an Ando trademark. All artwork is by Saskia Pintelon.
Far left: A connecting ramp and stair link the principal blocks in the spatial composition.
Left: The artist's materials alongside with the architect's monochrome palette.

Opposite top: A triangular vertical circulation space.
Opposite bottom: The formal dining area. Tadao Ando's work emphasizes the interplay of natural light and space.

smiles and chuckles. "Nobody had a clue how to produce concrete of the required quality," he admits, "and a huge number of electrical outlets had to be accurately positioned before the walls were cast. So we set out to acquire the knowledge. My colleague Ravindu 'Ravi' Karunanayake was central to the process and the structural engineer and contractor went to Japan to learn how to cast to the required standard." Two Japanese specialists, Kiyoshi Aoki and Yukio Tanaka, flew out from Japan to oversee the process of casting. When asked if this project has influenced later work, he concedes that "what this process has given us is a proven reputation for being able to produce high-quality work."

The residence provokes several responses, as it is a house of many moods. The terrace provokes elation and exhilaration, but also feelings of peace and solitude. The powerful geometry speaks of man's (temporary) power over nature in the way it is imposed on the land. But, for all the building's strength I reflect on man's tenuous grasp on the natural world. The house has a severe beauty. Concrete, grey tiles and polished cement provide a neutral backcloth for artworks. The play of natural light with space is characteristic of his work. "In all my works, light is an important factor," says Ando," I create enclosed spaces mainly by means of thick concrete walls. The primary reason is to create a place for the individual, a zone for oneself within society."[2]

Pringiers House is an exquisite piece of modern residential architecture that brilliantly meets the needs of its artist client.

[1] The painting 'Weligama Bay 2010' hangs in Koenraad Pringiers' house, Villa Vista, in the reception area (see page 104).
[2] Tadao Ando quoted in archdaily.com.

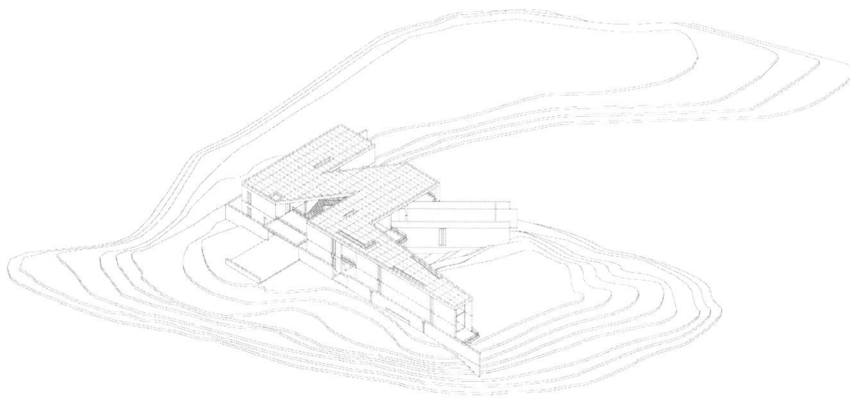

AERIAL PERSPECTIVE

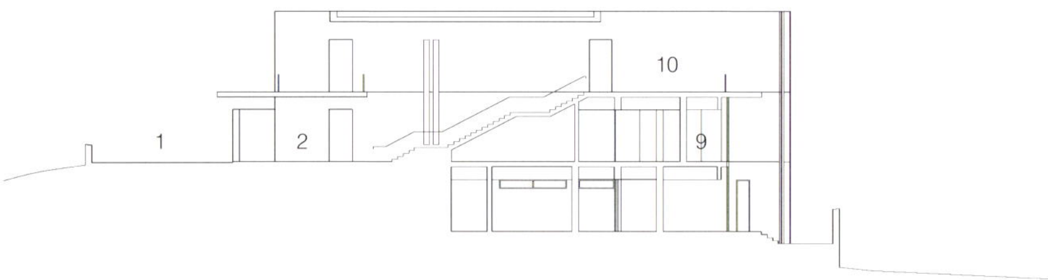

SECTION

1	Drop Off	9	Bathroom
2	Entrance Court	10	Sun Deck / Breakfast Area
3	Artist's Studio	11	Pool Deck
4	Living	12	Swimming Pool
5	Dining	13	Master Bedroom
6	Office / Study	14	Master Bathroom
7	Elevator	15	Gallery
8	Bedroom		

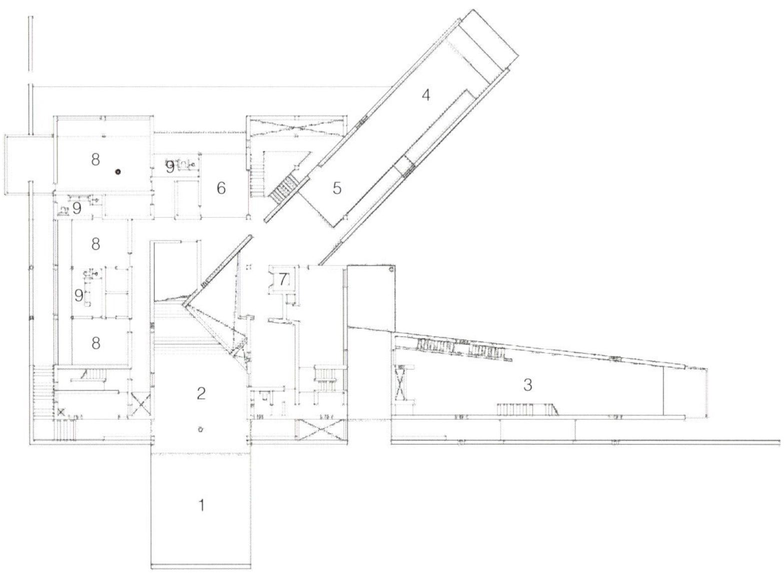

GROUND FLOOR PLAN

0 5M 10M 20M

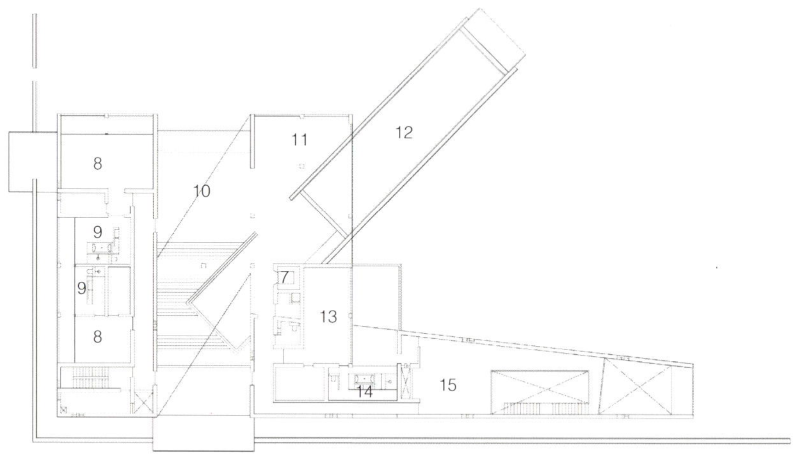

FIRST FLOOR PLAN

Opposite: The master bathroom suite with a view to Weligama Bay.
Left: The ascent to the upper court is charged with growing anticipation of the view beyond.

Saffrons Beach House

Habaraduwa

Architect	Philip Weeraratne and Ravindu Karunanayake *PWA Architects*

Saffrons Beach House was initially designed for an Australian couple who worked in the media. They had planned to spend their retirement years by the Indian Ocean but, when one of them fell ill, they returned to Australia and ownership passed to a family from Hyderabad, India who visit regularly.

The two-storey, four-bedroom beachfront house is sandwiched between the Matara Road and the beach. It is essentially a layered rectangle with a low-pitched roof parallel to the road and facing the white sandy beach. The layer closest to the road consists of the kitchen courtyard and staff accommodation, the house entrance and entrance court, a two-car garage and a courtyard serving the fourth bedroom. The purpose of this 'outer' layer is to exclude noise and traffic pollution.

The second layer consists of open-to-sky courts, a linear koi pond and the principle staircase. The intention is to further distance the main living spaces from traffic pollution. The third layer consists of the principle living spaces — the dining/living room, the master bedroom suite and two of the remaining bedrooms. The final layer is a south-facing verandah protected by wide eaves and horizontal louvres at first-floor level.

A garden, shaded by tall coconut palms, lies to the south and east of the house with a shimmering pale blue swimming pool and a pool deck on the western boundary. In the southeast corner of the garden is an atap-roofed spa pavilion and separating the private space from the narrow white public beach and the breakers of the Indian Ocean is a low belt of mangrove vegetation.

Upon entering the house from the road the view of the sea is delayed by the configuration of the entrance. One moves from the entrance lobby into a generous courtyard and then across a bridge spanning a linear koi pond and eventually to a foyer facing the beach. A waterfall cascades into the pond alongside an open-riser staircase. The choreography in this unfolding drama is brilliant.

The house is a joyous place where bright-coloured fabrics contrast vividly with the predominantly white, grey and black monochrome architecture. The entrance court is particularly striking, for it is painted a rich golden

Previous page: The pool and pool deck viewed from the garden. At dusk candles are placed in the recesses in the concrete wall and their flickering light dances on the pool.
Above: Looking north over the pool to the Indian Ocean. A daybed on the pool deck overlooks the activity on the beach.
Opposite: The expertly layered façade of the house reduces solar heat gain.

yellow emulating the crocin dye obtained from the saffron plant, the world's most costly spice. The design exhibits the confident manipulation of light and space. The location of light and air wells is very astute and ensures the circulation of air. Southwest-facing sliding doors and windows are clear glass without frames giving the impression of being outdoors. "This is an effect we wanted to create," explains the architect, "one of bringing the outdoors in." It is achieved without the attendant problems of heat gain for the windows are well shaded.

The architect of Saffrons Beach House, Philip Weeraratne, worked closely with his colleague Ravindu Karunanayake to produce a high quality home. Weeraratne studied architecture in the part-time course at the City School of Architecture (CSA) in Colombo from 1987 to 1995. "The City School of Architecture had only just started and there was tremendous energy. Geoffrey Bawa used to arrive in his white Rolls Royce. I was in the second batch of students on the part-time course. I met C Anjalendran in my first year and he expanded my horizons. Without him I believe I may not have continued my studies in Sri Lanka as my mother was promoting study in the USA but I wanted to maintain the link with Anjalendran."

Saffrons Beach House was shortlisted for a Geoffrey Bawa Award in 2007. Building commenced in 2002 and although work stopped in the aftermath of the 2004 tsunami, the house was finished soon thereafter. It predates the architect's collaboration with Tadao Ando and Shigeru Ban (see pages 108–115 and 100–107). The qualities of this house possibly clinched their invitation to be the local Architect of Record.

"Expatriates bring in new ways of thinking," says Weeraratne, reflecting on the original client's brief. "The Australians wanted the house to be modern and they did not want 'vernacular style'. They were insistent upon, and were prepared to pay for, materials that would not deteriorate given the high humidity, the saline levels and the dangers of corrosion." As a result, the holiday home looks much the same today as when it was built nearly a decade earlier.

Opposite: An open riser staircase ascends over the linear pond. The water assists in cooling the interior.
Right: The double-height dining area with bright tryptich on wall.
Below: The house is one room wide, a key factor in facilitating natural ventilation.

Left: A sweeping vista of the house and garden from the far side of the swimming pool. The sparkling pool, swaying palm trees and green lawn result in an archteypal tropical beach house feel.

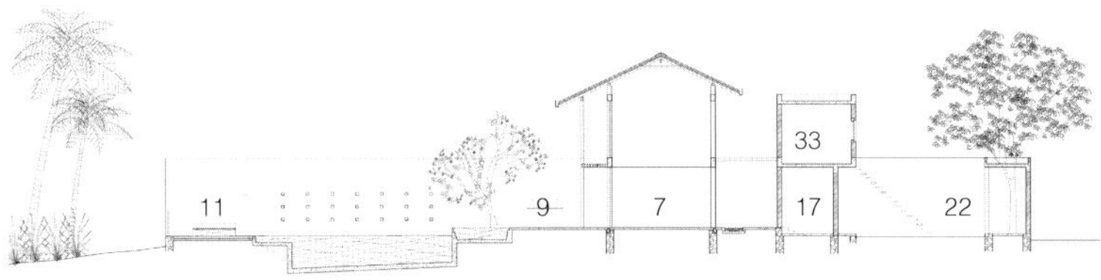

SECTION

1	Entrance	19	Kicthen Store
2	Vestibule / Corridor	20	Kitchen Store
3	Entrance Court	21	Driver
4	Bridge	22	Service Courtyard
5	Lobby	23	Garden Court
6	Living	24	Garden
7	Dining	25	Master Bedroom
8	Pond	26	Closet
9	Outdoor Dining	27	Master Bathroom
10	Pool	28	Bridge
11	Pool Deck / Bed	29	Bedroom
12	Bedroom	30	Study
13	Bathroom / WC	31	Terrace
14	Garage	32	Bathroom
15	Service Entrance	33	Staff Accomodation
16	Store	34	Beach
17	Kitchen	35	Roof Garden
18	Kitchen Store		

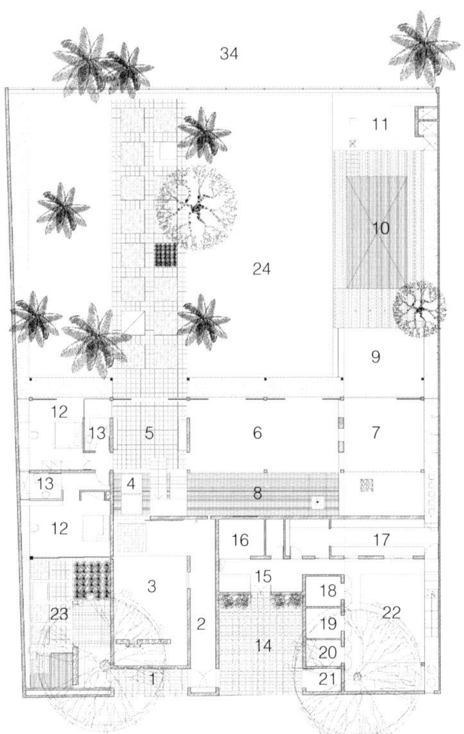

GROUND FLOOR PLAN

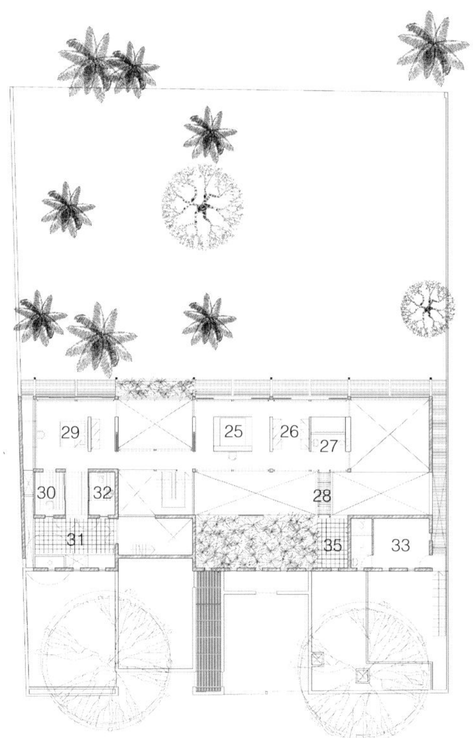

FIRST FLOOR PLAN

Above: A steel and timber bridge connects the master bedroom suite to a secluded roof garden.
Right: The master bathroom and closet with views out to the ocean.
Far right: A narrow entrance vestibule delays the experience of the sudden explosion of light as one emerges in the lobby.

The Tamarind House

Battaramulla

Architect	Kumudu Munasinghe *PAN ARCH*

The Tamarind House is the home of architect Kumudu Munasinghe (45) and his family. Munasinghe graduated from the Department of Architecture at the University of Moratuwa in 1995 having worked for one year with C Anjalendran in1993. His teachers included Vijitha Basnayaka (see pages 192–199). Upon graduation he found employment as an architect working for the developer who was constructing Colombo's World Trade Centre designed by Hong Kong based Anthony Ng Architect. Later he worked on the Ceylinco Seylan Tower, also in Colombo, designed by Kerry Hill Architects.

Munasinghe's year with Anjalendran was influential for it gave him his first experience of practice and the

rigour required in planning a building. But Munasinghe affirms he has his own style: "I see tropical modernism in a different way. I prefer a minimalist style that suits Sri Lanka more. We are a tropical country and a lot of dust collects so you have to design a house very simply. Minimalist architecture is easy to maintain and it suits our lifestyle." Working on the Ceylinco building was also influential as he grew to appreciate the clean lines and reductionist details in Kerry Hill's design.

In 2000 Munasinghe set up practice as PAN ARCH with a British-born architect Sir Ian Jennings, a graduate of the Bartlett School of Architecture at University College London, who was formerly a director with Anthony Ng in Hong Kong, but who is now resident in Colombo.

The Tamarind House was completed in 2005 and is conceptually a response to the site that is located at the end of a short cul-de-sac in Battaramulla. It is a friendly neighbourhood, without high walls and iron gates, and children play cheerfully in the public space. The house may eventually lose a view towards trees to the north east when an adjoining site is developed, so the architect has predicted the outcome and turned the house inward to face a garden court. The plan was simultaneously 'twisted' to accommodate an existing mature tamarind tree. By manipulating and fragmenting the plan in this manner the architect has retained the view of the tree and the garden. The result is a composition with interlocking geometry and a meandering route through the various spaces. "I like minimalist architecture with simple lines and spaces," says Munasinghe, "my house uses cubic shapes focusing on the garden."

Kumudu Munasinghe's wife, Amitha Yapa, is also an architecture graduate of the University of Moratuwa and she effectively fulfilled the role of the client. The living room is a dramatic double-height space entered from the reception area and the dining area is accessed via a curved corridor. Both look into the garden court. Early

Previous page: The living room is an exhilarating double height space that is linked to the garden.

Opposite: The TV lounge has a plaster ceiling painted silver and a polished cement floor. The room overlooks the tamarind tree in the entrance court.

morning sunlight is problematic given the amount of glass and the height of the space in the living room, so blinds are employed to reduce the heat gain. Materials are mainly polished cement floors and, unusually, silver painted walls and ceiling with dark-stained timber highlights in selected locations. A stone tablet at the entrance to the house carries an excerpt from the *Dhammapada*, one of the best-known Buddhist scriptures.

The concept of a home office is incorporated in the plan. Attached to the house is a design studio above the triple-car garage. This accommodates six workstations and is accessed by a separate entrance from the arrival court, keeping work and home life separate.

Above: The living area with the principal staircase beyond defined by a concrete frame.

Left: A curved corridor connects the splayed cubist blocks that comprise the principal rooms.

Left: The architect has deftly maneuvered the house within a difficult site configuration and simultaneously retained a mature tamarind tree.
Below: A quiet corner of the master bedroom suite.
Opposite: The principal rooms in the house are skillfully orientated towards the pleasant south-facing garden court.

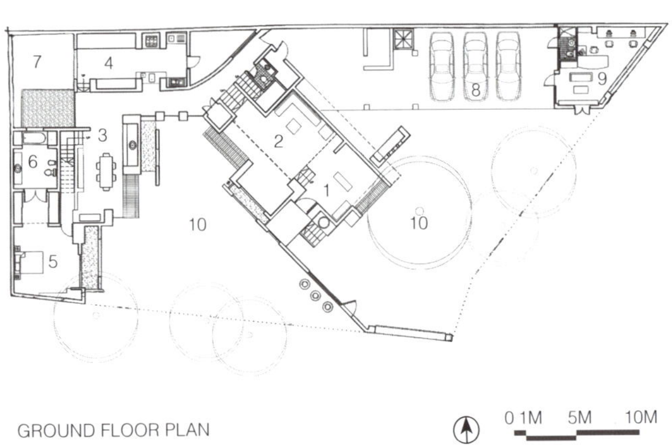

GROUND FLOOR PLAN

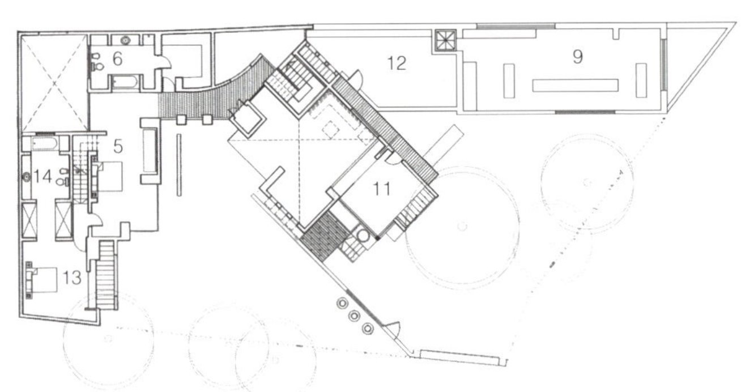

UPPER FLOOR PLAN

ELEVATION

1	Lounge	8	Car Park
2	Living Area	9	Office
3	Dining Area	10	Garden
4	Pantry	11	TV Lounge
5	Bedroom	12	Study Room
6	Bathroom	13	Master Bedroom
7	Courtyard	14	Master Bathroom

Channa Daswatte House

Madiwela, Kotte

Architect Channa Daswatte
MICD Architects

Architect Channa Daswatte has designed a remarkable house at Madiwela, for his own use. The house, completed in 2005, is an exposition of his way of life and a repository of memories. Born in Colombo, Daswatte grew up on a coconut plantation and as a young man his life moved back and forth between Trinity College, a boarding school in Kandy, and rural life in a village in the hill country. As a result Daswatte developed a deep understanding and respect for the landscape.

Later, he studied architecture at the Department of Architecture at the University of Moratuwa and graduated in 1987, proceeding two years later to the Bartlett School of Architecture at University College London, where he gained a Masters in 1991. Daswatte followed in C Anjalendran's footsteps and joined Bill Hillier's course on 'Space Syntax' where he investigated the social expression of space employing Hillier's groundbreaking methodology. He recalls one particular lecture by Hillier when he had 'a moment of revelation'. He enjoyed London and regards it as a second home.

The house is set in a hollow that was quarried to provide earth for the island on which the Sri Lankan Parliament building is located at Kotte. Enclosed by a high wall, it is accessed through a steel gate that leads to a vehicle court and garage from which shallow stairs and a ramp gradually ascend to the house. There is a roof garden above the garage.

The dwelling is a narrow rectangular two-storey pavilion on a northwest/southeast axis facing a garden that is the main focus of the house. The original intention was to place it on a northeast/southwest axis but *vastu* advice received from his partner Murad Ismail had it turned through 90 degrees. This works well with the sun's path and the predominant wind direction.

The house is arranged such that on arrival for a formal occasion guests ascend to the living space at first floor for pre-dinner drinks. There is also a library at first-floor level and the master bedroom suite with en-

Previous page left: The magical house viewed over the lap pool from the guest pavilion. The first floor shutters are thrown back to permit cool evening breezes.

Previous page right and left top: The dining room is open on both sides and looks out over the lush garden on one side.

Left below: The verandahs outside the twin guest pavilions.

Opposite: The architect's study and music room. The cushions are designs from fab India, Pakistani Ajrak prints and Sri Lankan Dumbara weaving.

suite bathroom. Pivoted shutters encircle the first floor and form a 'second skin'. The library has an inner skin of glass while the bathroom is open-sided and privacy is achieved by rotating the timber louvres. Since the plan form is only one room wide there is excellent natural ventilation. When the shutters are open at dusk the upper floor is remarkably transparent and sitting above the solid ground floor base it evokes the description 'Tropical Miesien'.

The kitchen is at the lower level along with a large open-sided dining space and an apartment for the architect's parents when they visit. The ground floor is a magnificent space that is the focus of everyday life. It spills out to the garden and pool with adjoining terrace. Facing the main house, across a lawn surrounded by tall trees are three guest rooms created by refurbishing a small house on the adjoining property that Daswatte acquired. Beyond the guest rooms is a tennis court in the high-sided quarry.

There is a wealth of history embedded in Channa Daswatte's house: the timber floors in the library and the master bedroom were salvaged from the demolished Coomaraswamy House in Albert Crescent, Colombo designed by Minnette De Silva and the ceiling in his bathroom is a mock-up made by Ena De Silva for a hotel in India designed by Daswatte. The timber louvred shutters that encircle the house at first-floor level were rescued from the Bentota Beach Hotel (a quintessential Bawa design) when its new owners refurbished the hotel. Subsequently Daswatte stored the shutters in his garage for many years waiting for an opportunity to reuse them. All the new doors and windows, manufactured from trees planted by his father at the time of Daswatte's childhood, were gifts from his parents.

Daswatte worked for C Anjalendran from 1988 to 1989, then joined Geoffrey Bawa in 1991 after finishing his Master's degree at the age of 26. His own house is inspired by Bawa, with elements of the Bentota Beach section evident. Daswatte finished off the projects in Bawa's office when his employer suffered a stroke in 1998. Afterwards, he branched out in partnership with another former Bawa employee, Murad Ismail, as MICD Architects. Ismail's own residence is on an adjoining site as is their office. Daswatte could have created a direct path to the office, but prefers to walk via the public road and to engage with the community.

The Channa Daswatte house is a powerful design statement. It is informed by scholarship and artistic skill. The house simultaneously connects to the past and looks to the future.

Above left: The dressing room with a planter's chair and hat stand.
Above right and opposite: The bathroom is open to the breezes and the sun and rain are mitigated by timber louvred shutters. The ceiling is a mockup made by Ena de Silva for a hotel in India that was designed by Channa Daswatte.

Above left: The timber louvred shutters were recycled from the Bentota Beach Hotel when it was undergoing renovation.
Above right: A ground-floor window where the architect eschews glass in favour of timber louvres.
Opposite: The architect/owner's comfortable living area at first-floor level.

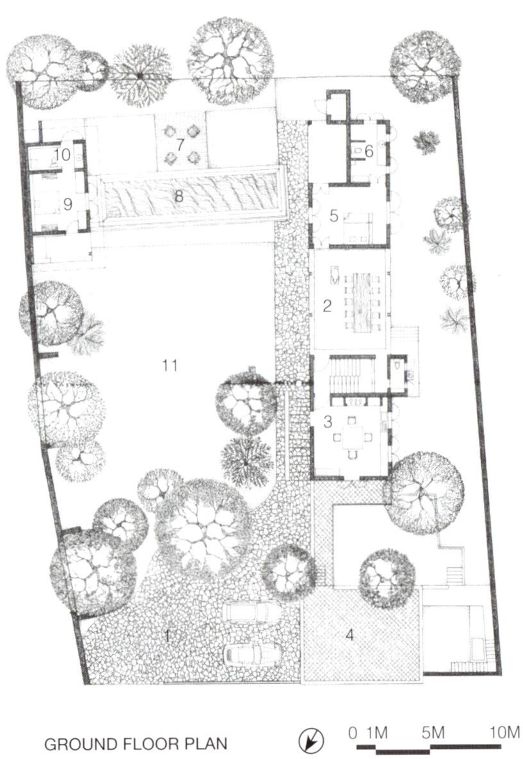

GROUND FLOOR PLAN

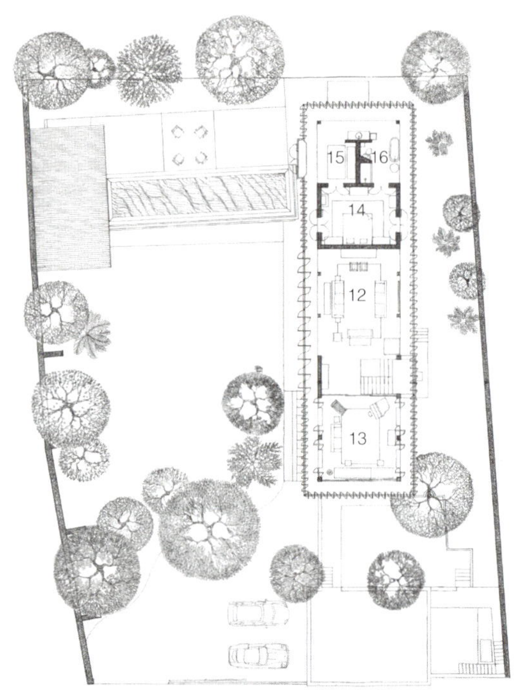

FIRST FLOOR PLAN

1	Entrance Court	9	Guest Pavilion
2	Dining	10	Guest Bath / WC
3	Breakfast / Kitchen	11	Garden
4	Roof Terrace	12	Living
5	Parent's Room	13	Library / Study
6	Parent's Bathroom / WC	14	Master Bedroom
7	Pool Deck	15	Closet
8	Swimming Pool	16	Master Bathroom / WC

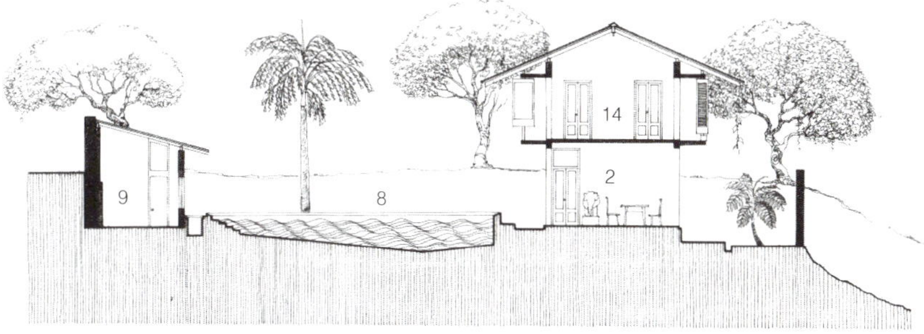

SECTION

Hettiarachchi House

Wattala

Architect **Vinod Jayasinghe**
Vinod Jayasinghe Associates

Located in Wattala, a suburb to the northeast of Colombo, the Hettiarachchi House is the home of the family of a botanist turned landscape designer and contractor. A modern two-storey residence with a tall water tower and a flat roof terrace, it is sited at the end of a cul-de-sac alongside a lush green paddy field. The rice is irrigated by a small watercourse that drains into the historic Dutch Canal, now largely overgrown but once used for the transportation of agricultural produce to the capital. The house is 'L'-shaped with its short leg projecting southwards and its long leg running westwards along the northern boundary. A high wall surrounds the house to keep out the crocodiles that are rumored to live in the canal.

The architect of the house is Vinod Jayasinghe (51), a 1994 graduate of the Department of Architecture at the University of Moratuwa. Jayasinghe was employed as an assistant to Geoffrey Bawa between 1987 and 1989 during the final years of the Edwards, Reid & Begg partnership. Among other projects, he worked on the design of the Royal Oceanic Hotel and he established a good working relationship with a number of Bawa's clients. Subsequently, he was commissioned to extend or refurbish several of his former employer's designs. His refurbishment of the Royal Oceanic Hotel in Negombo in 2003 — renamed the Beach Hotel — was achieved in a manner that Bawa probably would have applauded and in 2012 he gave a new lease of life to Bawa's Blue Lagoon Hotel at Talahena, now called the Jetwing Lagoon Hotel.[1]

The entrance to the Hettiarachchi House follows a carefully choreographed route from the southeast corner of the site, through a landscaped open-to-sky entrance court with a permeable louvred concrete screen wall that permits views of the paddy field. Two sharp right turns bring one to the entrance lobby looking west across a landscaped walled garden with several mature trees. Epiphytes cling to the off-form concrete structure and a small Catholic shrine marks the culmination of the entrance sequence. The principle staircase is neatly tucked away and stretching to the west along the longer 'leg' of the plan, is the glazed living and dining

area and an outdoor terrace with a steel pergola and a small pond. A guest bedroom with a private courtyard terminates the west wing.

Running parallel with the 'served' elements of the plan are the 'service' facilities, those back-of-house activities that ensure a house can function efficiently. Thus a separate entrance in the northeast corner of the site leads via staff accommodation to the kitchens, storage rooms, pantry and a service stair. The separate entrances are arranged on either side of the garage and a small office adjoins the parking space.

Ascending to the upper floor, there are three bedrooms all orientated towards the garden and the paddy field beyond the boundary wall. Solar panels have been placed on the roof and landscaping has commenced on the roof terrace.

The house is a bold orthogonal composition with a strong dialogue between interior and exterior. The architectural language combines off-form concrete, exposed steel columns and beams and large areas of clear glass in black timber frames of exceptionally high quality. However, when questioned, Jayasinghe will not be drawn on direct influences and suggests inspiration comes from many sources.

[1] Robson, David, 'The Beach Hotel, Negombo', in *Beyond Bawa*, Thames and Hudson, London, 2007, p169.

Previous page top left and bottom left: The elegant living and dining rooms stretch to the west, looking out over the walled garden.
Previous page bottom right: The living/dining wing viewed from the family lounge. Further to the west a pergola shades the patio.
Previous page right: A tall water tower provides a counterpoint to the two-storey orthogonal composition.

Opposite: The master bed-room overlooks the garden and the patio.
Below: The family lounge – an outdoor verandah that connects directly to the garden and is a prelude to the living room.
Right: Off-form concrete columns support the water tower and provide a surface for the propagation of epiphytes.

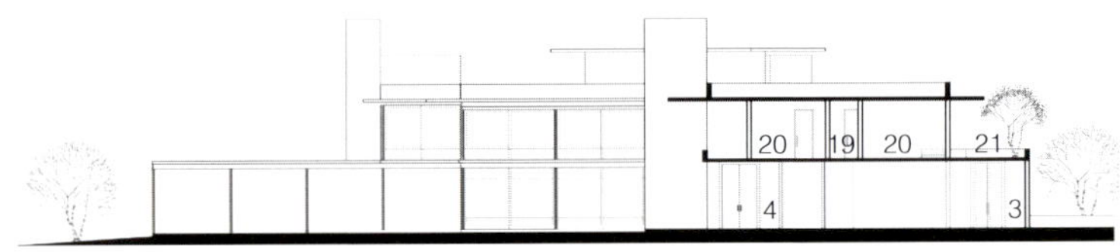

SECTION

1	Entrance Foyer	12	Servant Room
2	Main Entrance	13	Servant Toilet
3	Visitors' Lounge	14	Garage
4	Family Lounge	15	Office
5	Living	16	Powder Room
6	Dining	17	Family Living
7	Patio	18	Master Bedroom
8	Kitchen	19	Bathroom
9	Guest Bedroom	20	Bedroom
10	Bath Room	21	Roof Garden
11	Courtyard	22	Courtyard Below

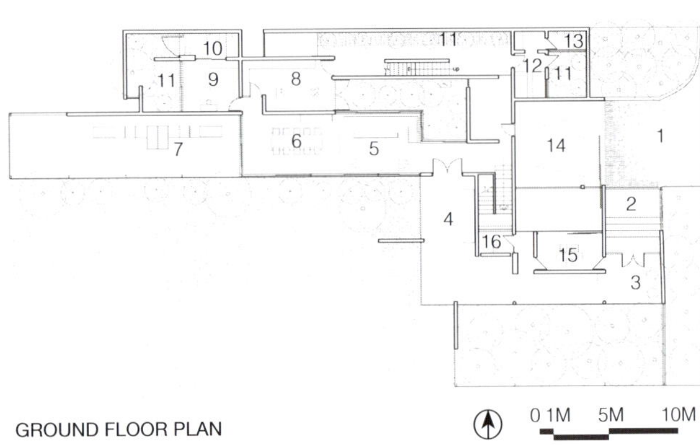

GROUND FLOOR PLAN

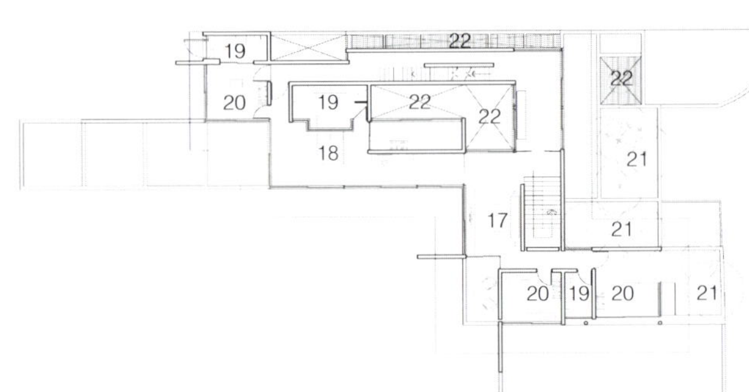

FIRST FLOOR PLAN

Opposite: A view from the master bedroom to the verandah that forms the family lounge area.
Above: Sliding/folding timber shutters separate the master bathroom from the master bedroom. They can be opened to connect the two spaces and enhance cross ventilation.
Left: A linear service courtyard runs parallel to the principal rooms in the house.

The Urban Slice House

Rajagiriya

Architect Palinda Kannangara

The Urban Slice House is an enchanting residence in Royal Court, a gated complex on the eastern fringe of Colombo. The house, designed for a businessman and his family, is one of the first dwellings in the new development and will eventually be flanked by others. For now it stands as a rectangular high-walled stone enclosure, inside which is a glass 'jewel' of a dwelling. It is almost as if one were opening a hard 'shell' to find a glittering pearl within.

The architect is Palinda Kannangara (44), a graduate of the seven-year part-time course in architecture offered by the City School of Architecture within the Sri Lanka Institute of Architects (SLIA). He was employed by Anura Ratnavibhushana for six years from 1998 to 2004 and he obtained his practice license in 2004.

The owners of the Urban Slice House knew of Kannangara's modernist credentials and wanted a contemporary house, but they also wanted it to be 'homely', a brief that provided a challenge to Kannangara's ingenuity. The house is entered through a stone entrance porch, on a central axis that is orientated north to south. The façade reveals little of the interior layout with a stone base and timber louvres concealing a balcony at first-floor level. To the east upon entering is the garage, to the west a landscaped entrance courtyard and a two-storey reception space with large glazed openable windows. Directly ahead is the dining area, looking west into a second, open-to-sky, red gravel surfaced courtyard. To the left, across a linear pond, is the pantry and to the rear of the house the kitchen and staff rooms. A powder room and a bedroom for a guest or elderly relative completes the ground floor accommodation overlooking a third courtyard that extends to the southern boundary wall of the site.

At the heart of the plan is a dramatic open-riser staircase that extends to roof level and is capped by a glass box to prevent rain penetrating. The vertical

circulation ascends from the dining area to the first floor emerging at the family room with direct access to the master bedroom and two smaller bedrooms. The family room looks west through vertical timber louvred shutters into the courtyard and both bedrooms at the rear of the house have views south into the rear courtyard while the master bedroom has a balcony with views north. Light penetrates into the core of the house via the stairwell and infuses every space with sparkling clarity. Natural ventilation is encouraged by the stack effect. The staircase continues up to the roof terrace where there is a spacious landscaped garden, ideal for al-fresco dining. It is a wonderfully cool place in the early evening with views to the south over rooftops. Perhaps it would benefit from a pergola to give shelter from the sun during the day.

What would otherwise be a pristine concrete and glass box with an orthogonal plan and interpenetrating volumes is softened by the introduction of timber louvred shutters and by bright red '*kadju*-coloured' furnishings. The lasting impression is of a sophisticated manipulation of space and light and the concept of duality in the planning where the exterior is robust and impassive while the interior is light and translucent.

Palinda Kannangara is an accomplished architect who in this project and The Leisure Pavilion (see pages 172–177) is making a substantial contribution to the development of a modern Sri Lankan architecture.

Previous page left: The house is entered directly into a stunning double-height living space with a walled courtyard beyond. The table contrasts recycled weathered timber railway sleepers with a stainless steel frame. **Previous page right:** The entrance façade – an elegant composition in stone, timber, concrete and glass. **Opposite:** An austere concrete staircase leads to the first floor. **Right, top:** The family room at first-floor level is a fusion of timber and red soft furnishings. **Right, centre:** The dining area alongside the courtyard is linked to the pantry via a bridge over a linear pond. **Right:** A dramatic open-riser staircase continues up to the roof terrace.

Above and left: The roof top pavilion and barbeque area with exhilarating views over the surrounding roofs.
Far left: The open-riser staircase ascends to the roof terrace.

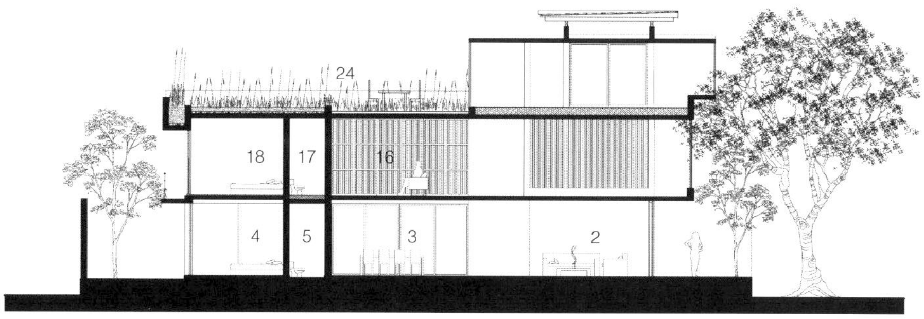

SECTION

1	Entrance Passage	13	Store
2	Living	14	Pond
3	Dining	15	Stairwell Lobby
4	Bedroom 1	16	Family Room
5	Toilet	17	Toilet 3
6	Timber Bridge	18	Bedroom 3
7	Pantry	19	Bedroom 4
8	Kitchen	20	Toilet 4
9	Service Passage	21	Master Bedroom Toilet
10	Servant Room	22	Walk In Closet
11	Toilet	23	Master Bedroom
12	Driver's Room	24	Terrace

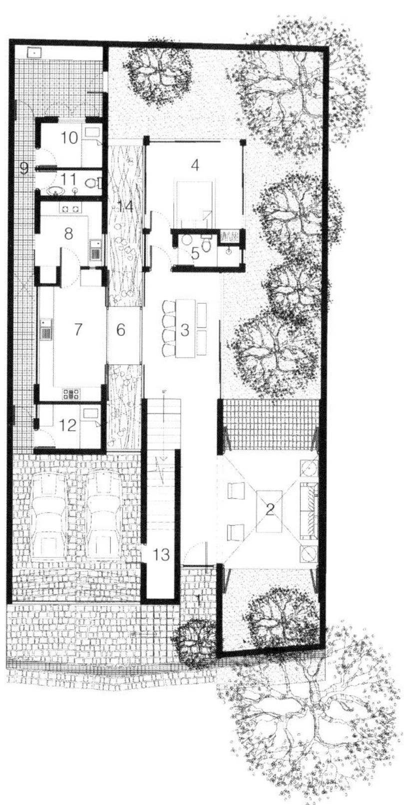

GROUND FLOOR PLAN

0 1M 5M 10M

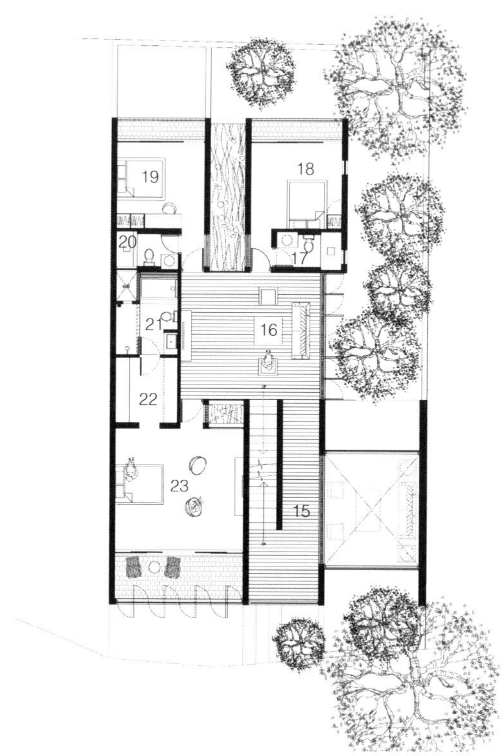

FIRST FLOOR PLAN

Amal & Himarsha House

Moratuwa

Architect Sudesh Nanayakkara

The Amal and Himarsha House is a marvelously compact suburban house with interlocking volumes assembled in the manner of a rubric cube around a glazed central lightwell penetrating through three floors. The owners are a much-travelled IT executive with an international bank and his wife, who works in the shipping industry. Their house is attached to her parent's home — the two units are directly connected at first-floor level and via a roof terrace to amalgamate into a 'three-generation dwelling'.

The architect is Sudesh Nanayakkara (36). Educated at the Department of Architecture, University of Moratuwa (1998 to 2007), his teachers included Madhura Prematilleke (see pages 62–69) and Vijitha Basnayaka (see pages 192–199). Nanayakkara worked with Vinod Jayasinghe Associates from 2002 to 2003

Previous page: The cool white interior of the house is enhanced by vertical shafts of daylight.
Left: A roof terrace connects the house to the adjoining residence of the owner's parents.
Opposite, left and bottom right: A shallow blue-green reflective pond greets the visitor on entering the house. The staircase has a protective grill.
Opposite top right: A lightwell provides daylight and ventilation to the bedrooms at first-floor level. A landsaped terrace connects the rooms.

and at Design Studio with Arosha Gamage from 2005 to 2007, returning for a further five years with Vinod Jayasinghe from 2007 to 2012. He gained his practice license in 2010 before setting up his own practice.

The house, completed in 2012, is entered via a hard landscaped entrance court, alongside a two-car garage. Moving diagonally across the courtyard and two steps up, one encounters the entrance lobby with a sparkling blue-green pond. An open-riser steel staircase ascends over the water flanked by a delicate perforated timber screen. Beyond is the living and dining room looking out to a narrow landscaped courtyard at the rear of the property. The walls are painted white and the floors are bleached timber. At the heart of the ground floor is a square landscaped courtyard below a deep lightwell that brings daylight and ventilation to the guest bedroom and the kitchen/servery.

At first floor there is a television room, two children's bedrooms, an ironing room, a family sitting room and, appropriately, a balcony linking the latter to the parents' dwelling with an external stair leading to a shared roof terrace. The central lightwell provides light to a sky court between the child's bedroom and the television room. The master bedroom occupies the second floor together with a large breezy roof terrace that is in effect a large outdoor room and recreation area.

Nanayakkara displays exceptional skill in the manipulation of interlocking volumes and spaces within a relatively small site area. The deep lightwell that penetrates to the ground floor brings a wonderful quality of daylight into the very heart of the home. The lightwell, together with permeable walls and screens, assists in naturally ventilating the internal spaces so that the house is delightfully cool without the use of air-conditioning. The architect shows a remarkable ability to design in cross-section and displays admirable restraint in the use of materials so that the house is an enchanting fusion of light and air.

The five-year-old practice is steadily building up a portfolio of hotels, commercial buildings and private hospitals to expand its residential work.

Above: A deep central vertical lightwell brings daylight to the courtyard at ground-floor level.
Right: The upper landing giving access to the roof terrace.
Opposite top: There are distant views of the ocean over the adjoining roofs.
Opposite bottom: The house is accessed directly from the street via a modest door.

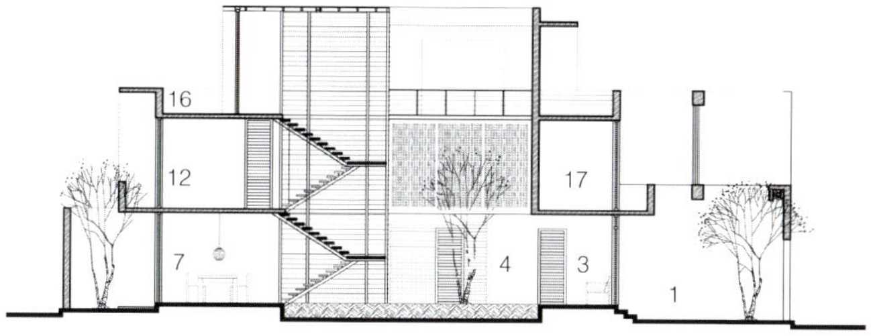

SECTION

1	Entrance	13	Bedroom
2	Garage	14	Courtyard
3	Lobby	15	Bedroom
4	Reflective Pond	16	Bathroom
5	Bathroom	17	Office
6	Bedroom	18	Maid's Toilet
7	Living	19	Utility
8	Dining	20	Maid's Room
9	Pantry	21	Terrace
10	Kitchen	22	Master Bedroom
11	Courtyard	23	Terrace
12	Family Living		

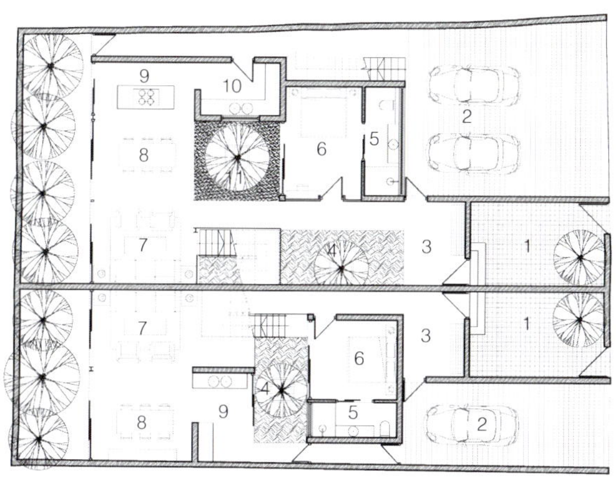

GROUND FLOOR PLAN 0 1M 5M 10M

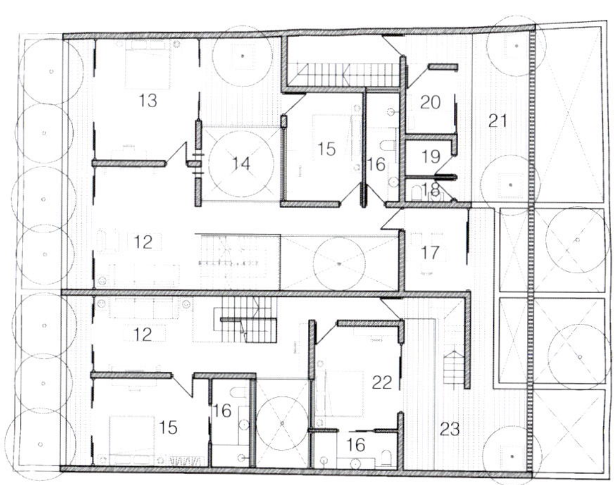

FIRST FLOOR PLAN

2B1

Mirihana

Architect Amila de Mel

2B1 is a startlingly original home built by and for Amila de Mel, an architect with an unconventional lifestyle that is encapsulated in the history of the house. De Mel had always yearned for a simple dwelling and in 1999 two six-metre (20-ft) shipping containers, previously used on a building site, were acquired and deposited on an empty site owned by her parents and in close proximity to her childhood home.[1] A large shed-like open-sided structure was then constructed with four trusses spanning over the containers — and vegetation was encouraged to grow up and over the roof.

The containers were insulated and made into a home and in 2004 the architect owner moved in. One container served as a bedroom and the other as a kitchen, dressing room and toilet. They were arranged in

a parallel configuration and separated by a timber deck. An open-to-sky bathroom was inserted between the kitchen/dressing room container and the boundary wall at the rear. Conceptually brilliant, in its initial incarnation the home was reputedly a great space for a party with an open-sided dining and living space completing the accommodation beneath the 'umbrella' roof.

Amila de Mel (50) began her initial training at art school in Boston, Massachusetts where she gained a BFA, prior to working with C Anjalendran for one and a half years (1989–1990) as one of the so-called 'verandah assistants' when he operated from his mother's house in Battaramulla. She was employed on a SOS Children's Village project. Later she joined Geoffrey Bawa and worked with the master architect for five years principally on the Kandalama Hotel before leaving in 1995 for further studies in architecture at the University of East London in the UK. In 1999 she was awarded her Dip. Arch. and returned to Sri Lanka where she set up her own practice in 2000. Her first client was Dominic Sansoni for whom she designed the Barefoot Garden Café. She is also the designer of Shirohana, a marvelous flower shop on Alfred House Road, for Rohan Jayakody.

De Mel sits on the Board of Habitat for Humanity, an international non-governmental and non-profit organization, which was founded in the USA in 1976 and began operating in Sri Lanka in 1994. The organization is devoted to building "simple, decent, and affordable" housing. In this role she is involved in a housing development programme funded by the Indian Government. The process of building her own house from recycled materials doubtless helped her in her role as a designer of affordable dwellings.

By 2010 the two containers had served their purpose as de Mel's temporary abode and were removed. A permanent single-storey structure was designed and built beneath the 'umbrella' replicating the footprint of the containers but with an extensive open-plan sitting 'room' on a first floor deck above the single-storey sleeping, bathing and kitchen facilities. An open kitchen is included and a delightful dressing room and open-to-sky bathroom. The creepers were pruned and a 'veil' of clear-glazed timber windows recycled from a demolished factory installed. Doors were brought from de Mel's grandfather's house and other recycled timber was utilized for floors.

In the process the house has lost none of its Bohemian character — and, in fact, is still evolving. The entrance is ambiguous for the floor of the living area is paved with bricks and part of the space is utilized as a car port. In 2010 de Mel added a guest room and a swimming pool in the northwest corner of the property. She has created a house that is close to nature where she can walk directly into the garden in the morning.

The curious tailpiece to this story of the experimental dwelling known as 2B1 is that it cannot be legally defined as a house because it does not have a front door. So it is still a storage space — a long-term temporary structure. And, apparently, it is still a great place for a party.

[1] The plan and pictures of the original house fashioned from shipping containers can be viewed in David Robson, *Beyond Bawa*, Thames and Hudson, London, 2007, p162.

Previous page: The heart of 2B1 is an extraordinary open living and formal dining space overlooked by a sitting room and recreation area.
Opposite and left: The semi-industrial appearance of the interior gives the house a quality of impermanence that is simultaneously intriguing and delightful.
Above: The modest kitchen/breakfast area contrasts with the soaring quality of the principal living space.
Overleaf: The exterior of the house is clothed in exuberant vegetation that from time to time has to be restrained.

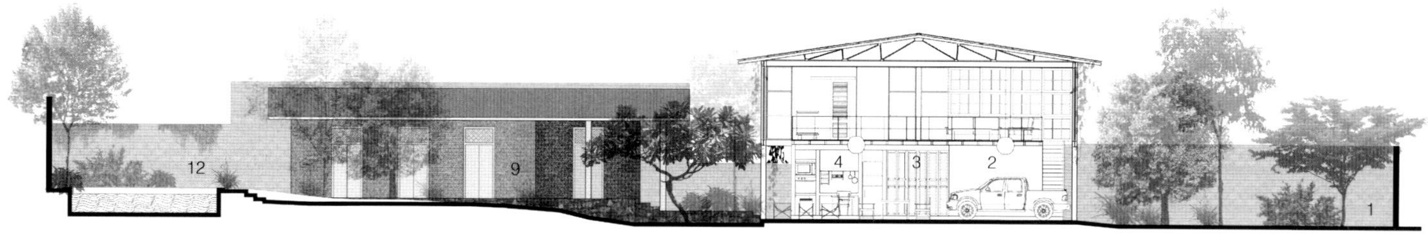

SECTION

GROUND FLOOR PLAN

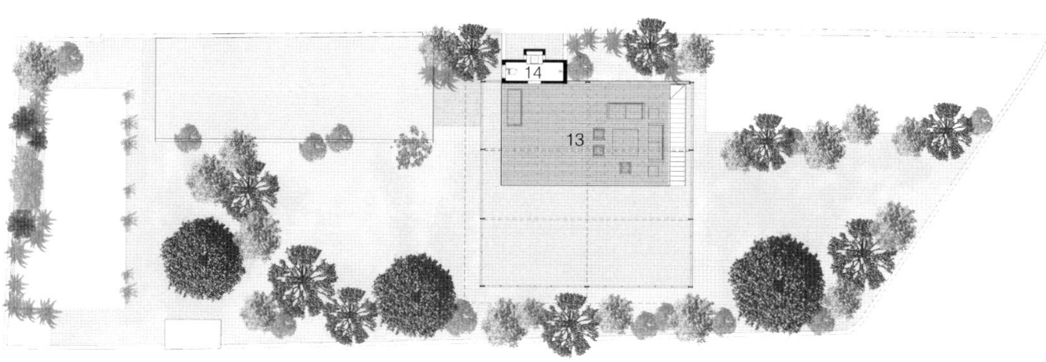

1	Entrance	8	Bathroom
2	Car port	9	Garden
3	Dining	10	Guest Room
4	Living	11	Guest Bathroom / WC
5	Kitchen	12	Swimming Pool
6	Bedroom	13	Sitting / Recreation Deck
7	Closet	14	Guest Toilet

FIRST FLOOR PLAN

Malalasekara House

Borella, Colombo 08

Architect C Anjalendran

The Malalasekara House, is a large urban house on a substantial 760-square-metre plot in Borella, Colombo, designed for a family involved in international trade and development who entertain at home and frequently have guests. The architect has disaggregated the extensive brief into smaller elements in order to mitigate the size of the dwelling. Thus, the public, family, guest and domestic areas are discreetly segregated in plan and section. The house in this sense follows the Louis Kahn maxim of functional separation of 'served' and 'service' spaces.[1]

The architect of the house is C Anjalendran (63). One of Sri Lanka's most notable architects, Anjalendran was awarded a BSc by the Department of Architecture at the University of Moratuwa in 1973 (the first by the

Previous page: The main house and guest pavilion viewed from the garden. A walkway with clay tiled roof links the two blocks. **Above:** The lightwell at the heart of the house ensures light and ventilation reach the deepest parts of the plan. **Right:** A view from the balcony outside the master bedroom. The batik wall hanging is a Korale Banner showing the sun and moon by the Aluwihare Cooperative of Ena de Silva and is a replica of batiks produced by the same artist that are hanging in the Sri Lankan Parliament building designed by Geoffrey Bawa. **Opposite:** The layered façade with deep overhanging eaves ensures that sun and rain are effectively prevented from reaching the house interior.

Department) and went on to study at the Bartlett School of Architecture, University College London where he was awarded a post-graduate Diploma in 1976 and a MSc in Spatial Morphology under Bill Hillier in 1979. He joined the practice of Edwards, Reid & Begg in 1978 as an assistant to Geoffrey Bawa. He left two years later and remained a close friend and confidante of Bawa until the architect's death in 2003. Anjalendran set up his own office in 1982 and speaks of Bawa with great reverence and respect as a master architect from whom he learned much.

The Malalasekara House is entered in the southwest corner through a relatively modest doorway on Tickle Road, into a 'chicane' entrance hall, which leads past a four-car garage that is concealed by a perforated screen. Directly ahead is a wide straight stair giving access to the private family domain at the upper level and beyond an expansive view over a koi pond towards the garden. To the left is a two-storey lightwell that brings light and ventilation into the centre of the house. The more public areas of the house comprising a large reception area and formal dining area are located beyond the lightwell and look northeast into the high-walled garden. Sliding doors, usually left open during the day, lead to a two-storey verandah and air is drawn across the sitting room by a stack effect in the lightwell.

The verandah leads via a short colonnaded walkway to a two-storey guest pavilion in the northeast corner of the garden that also houses an office on the ground floor. In this manner guests and business acquaintances can bypass the most private areas of the house. In the guest pavilion there are two bedrooms behind a deep verandah.

The northwest corner of the house is devoted to driver's accommodation, a service entrance, a service courtyard, and wet and dry kitchens with storage space. Domestic staff accommodation is accessed via a service stair in the northwest corner of the site that connects up to rooms at second-floor level.

The private accommodation of the house is all located at first-floor level and includes a sitting room with a ceiling extending up to the rafters, a master bedroom suite and bedrooms for two children with ensuite bathrooms. The master bedroom looks over the garden while the children's bedrooms and a study room look

over the street. All the rooms surround the tall lightwell that becomes, in effect, a courtyard in the sky.

I have explained the layout at some length for it serves to demonstrate how brilliantly Anjalendran arranges the relatively complex brief to enable different functions to take place simultaneously without conflicting. The most private family areas are carefully separated from the most public and miraculously woven into this 'living tapestry' is the idea of visual connections and an illusion of space. In addition, the section is brilliantly handled to achieve natural ventilation.

Also in evidence is the idea of 'double screens' extolled by Anjalendran and perimeter courtyards that are all part of a language handed down by Bawa. There are discreet links between the house and an adjoining property to the south owned by the parents of the family. Wide overhanging eaves are part of Anjalendran's stock-in-trade along with internal light- and airwells and abundant vegetation.

Anjalendran, along with his clients, has sourced artifacts and pictures for the house. Details include timber and stone columns recycled from demolished buildings; a brass sculptural piece in the reception area by the artist Laki Senanayake; an Ena De Silva batik flag, one of six originally commissioned for an exhibition of Geoffrey Bawa's work held in Frankfurt in 2004, and numerous paintings by Sri Lankan artists. The architect, who is an outspoken advocate of robust detailing in the tropical climate, has also sourced and reproduced traditional brass ironmongery throughout the house which contrasts and accentuates the teak doors and windows.

[1] Louis Kahn was concerned with creating strong formal distinctions between served spaces and service spaces. What he meant by service spaces was spaces such as stairwells, corridors, restrooms, or any other back-of-house function like storage space or mechanical rooms.

SECTION

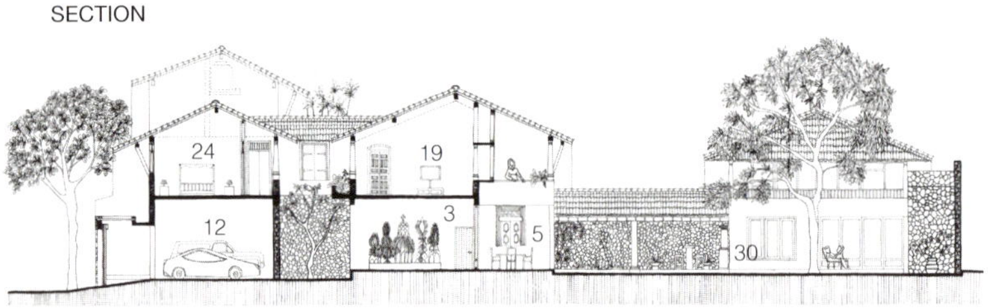

1	Lobby	11	Bath / WC	21	Master Bathroom
2	Reception	12	Garage	22	Closet
3	Living	13	Kitchen Court	23	Balcony
4	Dining	14	Staf Dining	24	Bedroom
5	Terrace	15	Driver's Room	25	Study
6	Kitchen / Breakfast	16	Service Entrace	26	Guest Bedroom
7	Storage	17	Staff Toilet / Bath	27	Staff Bedroom
8	Kitchen	18	Pond	28	Service Room
9	Guest Lounge	19	Family Room	29	Bathroom / WC
10	Office	20	Master Bedroom	30	Garden

GROUND FLOOR PLAN

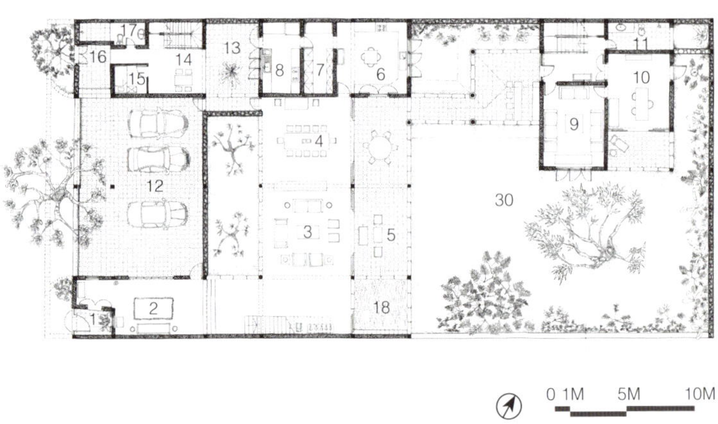

FIRST FLOOR PLAN

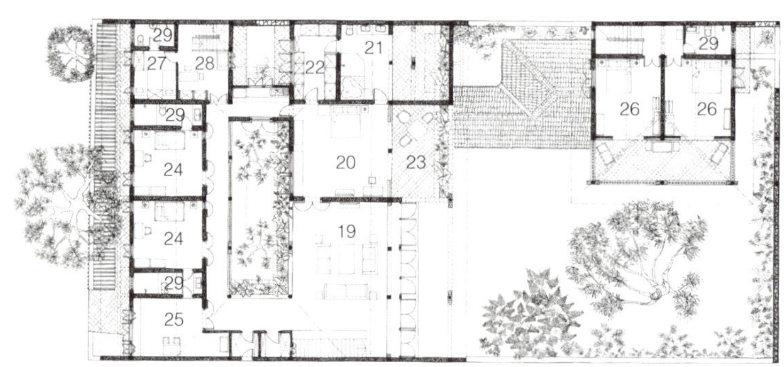

Previous page left and right: The living and formal dining areas are demarcated by a sculpture 'Abstract Forest' by the renowned Sri Lankan artist/sculptor Laki Senanayake. The room is just one room wide, which promotes cross ventilation when the sliding doors are open.
Opposite: The house is exquisite when viewed from the garden at dusk.
Left: The lofty master bedroom is an impressive space. The Turkoman carpet was purchased from Dhanak, a shop in Colombo.

The Leisure Pavilion

Colombo 03

Architect Palinda Kannangara

The Leisure Pavilion is an audacious building in a dense urban location in Colombo. Essentially an entertainment pavilion, it provides a venue for parties because the owner's main dwelling, some ten minutes away by car, is judged not large enough for that purpose. In effect the 'public' side of his house has been transported to a site a short distance away from the 'private' activities of the family. The brief gave the architect, Palinda Kannangara (44), free reign to exercise his imagination and the result is a minimalist garden shelter — a magical place devoid of all physical manifestations of the owner's personal life.

It is very clever, for all too often we have to negotiate public and private life in a congested space.

Born in Colombo in 1970, Kannangara was educated at Ananda College, Colombo and went on to the University of Colombo. An accomplished mathematician, he graduated with a BSc in Physical Sciences in 1996. Whilst pursuing his university course he simultaneously studied architecture and signed up for the seven-year part-time course that was offered by the City School of Architecture within the Sri Lanka Institute of Architects (SLIA). Channa Daswatte taught in the school for two years while Kannangara was a student and C Anjalendran taught history. There was a symbiosis between the staff and students and many good architects came through the system.

Kannangara graduated in 2003 and obtained his license in 2004. During this time he worked for Professor Yamuna Ganeshan and Karthi Ganeshan from 1994 to 1996; with architect Vinod Jayasinghe from 1996 to 1998 and with architect Anura Ratnavibhushana from 1998 to 2004, at which juncture he set up his own practice.

Kannangara's architecture has been said "to focus on aesthetic and spatial exploration within the contemporary Sri Lankan context. He respects tradition without being restricted by it. He is drawn to a minimalistic design vocabulary, which is very much a part of Sri Lankan ethos, and his architecture is informed by his background in Mathematics and Art".[1]

The Leisure Pavilion is inspired by vernacular architecture in Sri Lanka. It is, in the architect's words, "a contemporary interpretation of an *ambalama*, a roof over a resting place, with scenic views". The

materials were the outcome of the client's expertise in hydroconstruction[2], thus concrete was preferred. It is calm, still and harmonious, employing an impressively simple concept of a large white rectangular portal with four intermediate concrete columns, within a compound surrounded by 4.8-metre-high, off form concrete walls and animated by sunlight. The ground plane is divided laterally into three sectors — grass, polished cement and more grass.

Approximately 65 percent of the walled urban compound is a lawn with two magnificent trees — one a large mango tree, the other an equally splendid banyan that hugs the concrete perimeter wall along the street façade. The concrete arch or portal is 6.6 metres high and almost 20 metres in length and extends over half of the remaining site area, sheltering the entertainment space which consists of a simple polished cement floor that is open to the elements on two sides.

In the southwest corner of the site there is a discreet entrance consisting of a 'hole in the wall' ledged and braced wooden door, a small bar, toilets, and a staff room clad in undressed timber planks with a staircase giving access to an upper level deck and koi pond. A second, wider, timber door in the northwest corner of the site provides access for the larger accoutrements of a party.

The Leisure Pavilion is the ultimate multi-purpose space and it has many moods. During the day it is a marvelously calm and contemplative place for meditation, almost monastic in its isolation from the busy city beyond the walls. Its appearance to the outside world is understated and self-effacing. At night the space takes on an entirely different persona when it transforms into an enchanting party venue with perimeter wall lights.

Originally designed for a client in the hydro-electrical power industry, based in Sri Lanka but doing projects in Kenya, who simply wanted to put something on the site, "to relax and entertain, a place of leisure for his family and guests," the pavilion was sold in 2013. Now, Palinda Kannangara faces the exciting challenge of adapting this magical place into a family home for its new owners. Those who admire the present building, which was the recipient of a Sri Lanka Institute of Architects Award for Excellence, eagerly await its reincarnation.

[1] www.masaassociation.com
[2] Hydroconstruction refers to the construction of concrete dams, ports, retention ponds and wells.

Previous page left: A box within a box. The minimalist lines of the portal frame viewed from the garden.
Previous page right: From the street nothing is revealed of the purpose of the Leisure Pavilion, merely an understated 'hole in the wall' entrance.
Opposite: The simple off-form concrete structure is a place for quiet reflection by day and a space for revelry by night.
Above left and right: The koi pond and fixed timber seating at the upper deck level.

Above: The pavilion is a convivial space for an informal meeting.
Right: A window to the bar area doubles as a serving hatch.
Far right: A shallow flight of stairs ascends to the upper deck.
Opposite: The service entrance ramp and an 'abandoned' canoe.

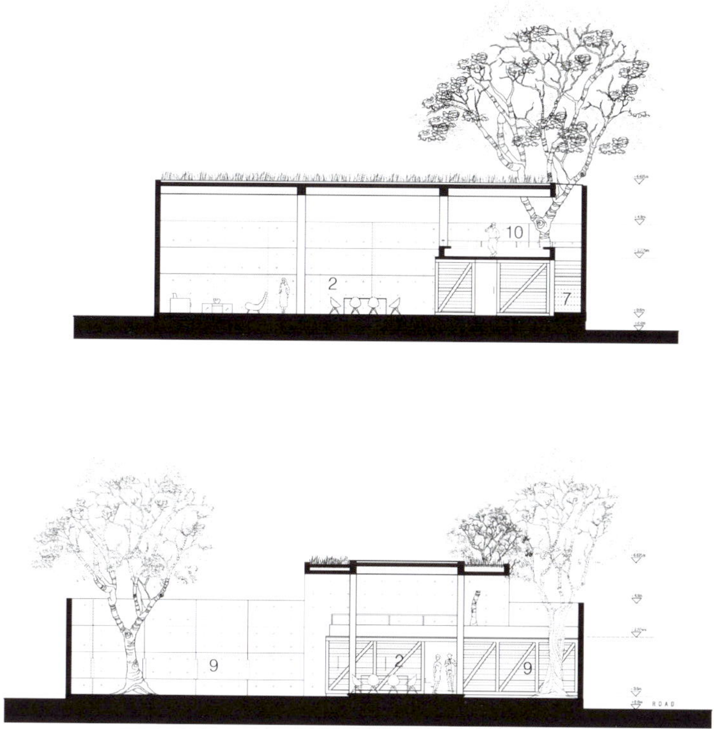

SECTIONS

1	Entrance Passage	7	Garden Tool Room
2	Living / Dining	8	Service Entrance
3	Pantry	9	Garden
4	Bathroom	10	Lounge
5	Toilet	11	Pond
6	Caretaker's Room		

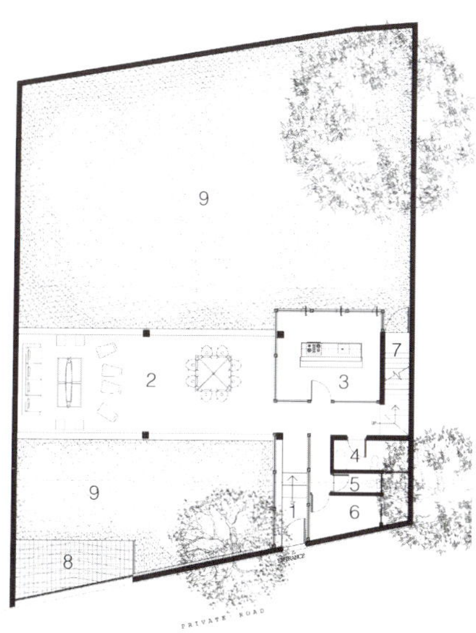

GROUND FLOOR PLAN 0 1M 5M 10M

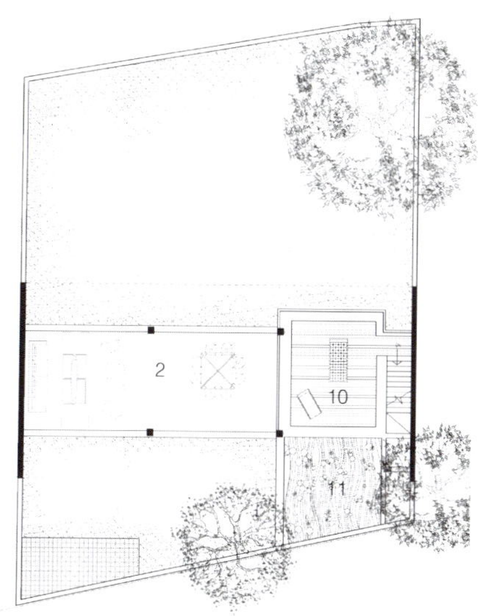

FIRST FLOOR PLAN

The Garden House

Colombo 07

Architect	Channa Daswatte *MICD Architects*

The Garden House is the dramatic city residence of two lawyers, one also an investment banker, and their three children. The term 'dramatic' is used intentionally for some aspects of the house are analogous with a theatre, thus family life might be described as being enacted upon a 'stage'.

The architect of the extraordinary house is Channa Daswatte (49) who studied architecture at the Department of Architecture at the University of Moratuwa and graduated in 1987. He worked for two years for C Anjalendran before proceeding to the Bartlett School of Architecture at University College London, where he gained a Master's Degree in 1991. He then joined Geoffrey Bawa's practice where he worked for six years, becoming Bawa's principal

assistant. Daswatte finished off the projects in the office when Bawa suffered a stroke in 1998, then he branched out in partnership with another former employee — Murad Ismail — as MICD Architects.

The entrance to the house from the street is modest, a simple metal barred door set back from the pavement in a stone wall alongside an equally restrained garage door. But once within the entrance court, the scale changes spectacularly. Turning right one encounters double leaf timber doors, almost 4m high within a metal screen. The doors are approached across a radial pattern of paving and a moonstone just below the threshold. Beyond the doors, the grand scale continues in the form of a soaring, 8-metre-high lobby. The contrast between the modest entrance door and the lobby space is startling.

Equally dramatic is the view of the walled garden to the north. Indeed, one feels immediately drawn to the open space framed by the orthogonal concrete structure analogous with a proscenium arch. To the right of the entrance lobby is another spectacular feature — a 10-metre-high open-to-sky landscaped courtyard — while to the left of the lobby and two steps up is the stair and elevator lobby. The scale of the entrance is huge, but smaller details relate to the human scale: a swing hangs by chains from the structure and an impressive Laki Senanayake designed chandelier in the form of an inverted tree growing down from the ceiling graces the space.

Advancing further, on the right is the living area, a tall open-sided space that is naturally ventilated, and to the left the dining area, equally tall. Both can be

Previous page: The connectivity between the house interior and the garden is conveyed in the view from the living area to the dining area.
Above left: The entrance to the stairwell giving access to the upper floors is at right angles to the entrance lobby axis.
Above right: The stairwell.
Opposite: A blue green swimming pool extends north from the living area and ends at a concrete wall.

Left: Upon entering the house there is an exhilarating view from the 8-metre-high entrance lobby to the garden beyond. The chandelier was designed by Laki Senanayake.
Opposite: The garden extends vertically, colonising the north-facing façade of the house.

closed to the elements by discreet folding glass doors, but when left open these areas engage directly with the garden beyond. A blue/green lap pool stretches out from the living room along the eastern boundary.

The external paving continues through the lobby from the entrance to the garden and by this device the architect conveys the feeling that one is neither inside nor outside but the two are directly connected. The use of 'grasscrete' along the northern façade of the house enhances this inside/outside relationship and the manner in which vegetation grows up the concrete structure and over the pergola on the north-facing façade further blurs the boundary between interior and exterior. The extension of the stone and concrete external finishes into the interior adds to this ambiguity. Such is the openness of the house both in the horizontal plane and the vertical plane that there is an acute sense of living outdoors. The permeability also permits natural ventilation that is assisted by ceiling fans.

The theatre analogy continues at the first-floor level. Four bedrooms including the master bedroom suite are arrayed around the family room, which has an elevated view of much of the activity below. The staircase, too, looks down into the entrance lobby and courtyard and obliquely into the living area. The interpenetration of solid and void, point and plane, and space and light add to the drama.

At the second floor there is a fifth bedroom, a gym, a music room and an impressive double-height library with access to an extensive rooftop terrace. Here, built-in seating surrounded by rooftop planting makes for a pleasant evening entertainment area.

The deep rectangular plan form with a footprint of 21-metre-wide x 18-metre necessitated a strategy of internal courtyards with open-to-sky spaces to introduce light and ventilation. The resultant house is on a 'grand' scale — the entrance lobby could in a very different context be the portico for a horse-drawn carriage. But the prime focus of the residence and the element that defines it is the connection between the house and the garden. Vegetation grows up columns and over the trellised terrace wall. There is an acute sense of 'living in a garden'.

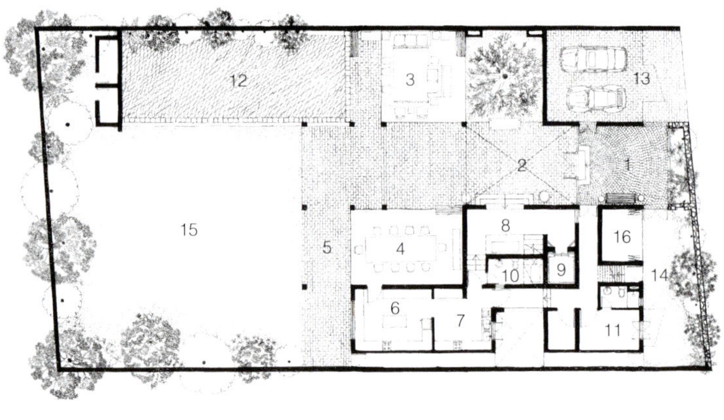

GROUND FLOOR PLAN

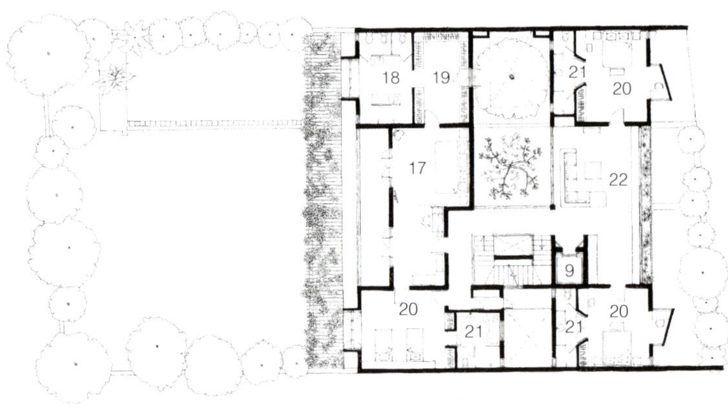

FIRST FLOOR PLAN

Opposite: At dusk the roof terrace offers a cool refuge.
Right: The impressive double-height library and music room at the second-floor level.

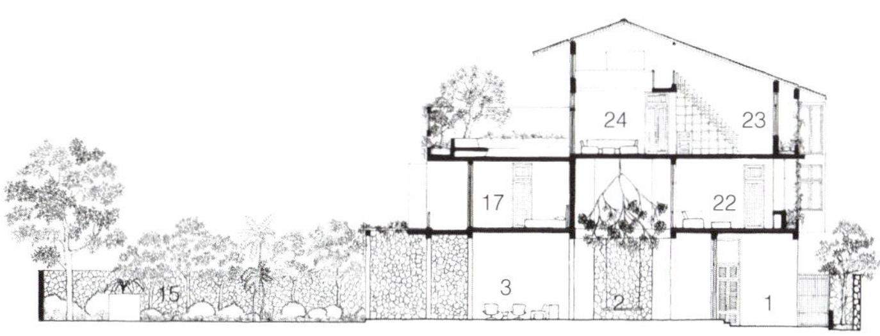

SECTION

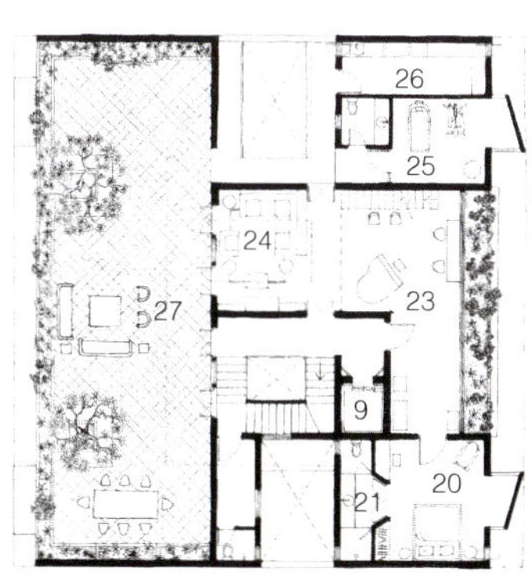

SECOND FLOOR PLAN

1 Entrance Court
2 Lobby
3 Living
4 Dining
5 Verandah
6 Pantry
7 Kitchen
8 Stair Lobby
9 Elevator
10 Powder Room
11 Staff Room
12 Swimming Pool
13 Garage
14 Service Court
15 Garden
16 Service Bay
17 Master Bedroom
18 Closet
19 Master Bathroom
20 Bedroom
21 Bathroom / WC
22 Family Room
23 Music Room / Libray
24 Lounge
25 Gym
26 Laundry
27 Roof Terrace

Samuel House

Colombo 03

Architect Godridge Samuel
mmGSarchitects

The Samuel House is a three-storey town house that is embedded in the city fabric and woven into the urban grain. It is the home of architect M M Godridge Samuel (52), his wife Beulah, a GP, and their three teenage children.

Samuel graduated from the Department of Architecture at the University of Moratuwa in 1991, receiving the SLIA Award for the highest overall marks in the MSc final examination and the Geoffrey Bawa Award for his final design project. Godridge recalls with a chuckle how in one studio review he was heavily criticised by Valentine Gunasekara who advised him pointedly not to do architecture. His success in the exams was a silent riposte. He obtained his license in 1992 and mmGSarchitects was established in 1998. A devout Christian, Samuel has since worked with the US Agency for International Development (USAID), the GOAL Humanitarian Organisation (an Irish NGO), CESVI (an Italian NGO), People in Need (a Czech Republic NGO), and the United Nations Children's Fund (UNICEF). Laudably, he has designed and built 60 schools, mostly in the eastern and northern provinces of Sri Lanka.

The Samuel House is entered via the carport into a linear reception and dining terrace that looks north west over a sunken landscaped garden. A wide roller shutter door is raised during the day so that the reception/dining area is completely open to the elements. "The roller shutter door was an important decision that allowed the terrace to be completely open but capable of being locked at night or partially lowered during a thunderstorm," Samuel explains.

At the heart of the plan are two parallel grey stone walls that define the vertical circulation and penetrate through three floors to a roof terrace. All the functions of the house are accessed from the central stair core. At ground level, in addition to the aforementioned reception and dining terrace, there is a kitchen with adjacent courtyard and a suite for the architect's mother. The master bedroom is at first-floor level along with a bedroom for one of the two teenage daughters, both

overlooking the high-walled garden court that is fringed with trees. To the south east of the stair core there is a second bedroom for the younger daughter and a family room. At roof level is another bedroom for a teenage son and a broad roof terrace facing north west that is used for entertainment purposes.

The green features of the house are exemplary: a central vertical ventilation shaft or 'chimney' provides natural ventilation by the stack effect, resulting in a remarkably cool interior, and solar panels on the roof ensure the electricity bill is zero. Indeed, Samuel is able to export power to the grid. Waste matter is composted and used to fertilise the garden where a pleasant walled orchard in the northwest corner is planted with mango, guava and banana trees in addition to *dang*, a local blueberry, and *jambu* or water apple. The orchard is a wonderfully silent place to sit or meditate.

There is a sense of self-sufficiency in this urban dwelling — it is akin to a citadel or bastion with its grey random rubble walls, the steel shutter and narrow staircases punctuated by lightwells and a steel walkway connecting the bedrooms at first-floor level. It is a house of contrasts between solidity and transparency and between darkness at the core and lightness at the periphery. Light filters into the interior through timber louvred shutters. There is distinct duality in the planning between the closed minimalistic appearance from the street and the openness when looking from the garden.

Previous page left: The view from the garden to the elevated living and dining terrace. The house is inward looking in its urban context.
Previous page right: A detail of the contrasting materials.
Above left and right: The compressed circulation spaces contrast powerfully with the openness of the garden and roof terrace.
Opposite top: The roof-top terrace offers a cool place for family members to congregate in the evening.
Opposite bottom left: A detail of the junction of a security grill with the stone façade.
Opposite bottom right: A delightful walled orchard provides a refuge for quiet contemplation and study.

Left, top and bottom: Throughout the house there is an interplay between darkness and light, and between compression of space and spatial explosion – it is the very essence of the architectural composition.

The house is a narrative with changing moods. Sky courts and niches punctuate the vertical 'processional route'. Samuel recounts how he has studied examples of urban form in Italy and Morocco and the manner in which dwellings are similarly woven into the urban fabric. "My earlier work was concerned with forms," he explains, "but now I work more with an architecture of space and light and movement through space."

One of the Samuels' daughters adds her critical appreciation when she says, "The house is cosy and airy and everyone has their own space, but it sometimes gets a little noisy. Then the orchard is a good place to study." The house deservedly received a SLIA Design Award in 2014.

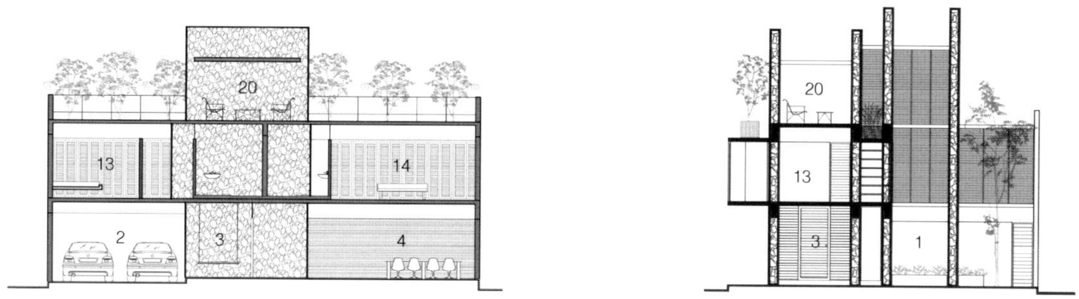

SECTION

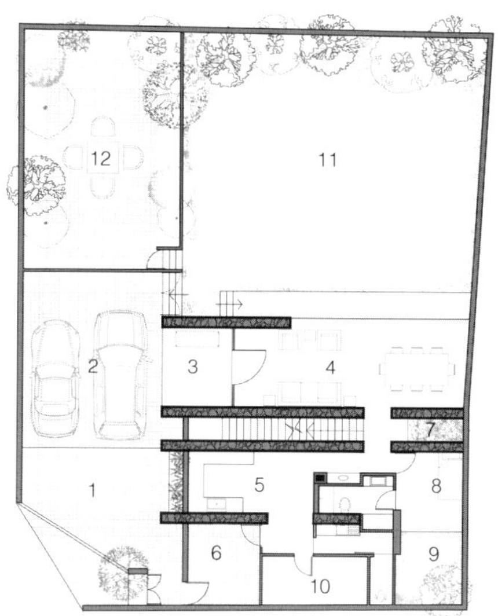

GROUND FLOOR PLAN

1	Entrance Forecourt	13	Master Bedroom
2	Car Port	14	Daughter's Room 1
3	Entrance Foyer	15	Steel Bridge
4	Living & Dining	16	Daughter's Room 2
5	Kitchen	17	Family Room
6	Kitchen Yard	18	Open-to-Sky Terrace
7	Ventilation Shaft	19	Roof Terrace
8	Mother's Room	20	Pavilion
9	Courtyard	21	Son's Room
10	Maid's Room	22	Store
11	Lawn	23	Roof Terrace (utility)
12	Mini Orchard		

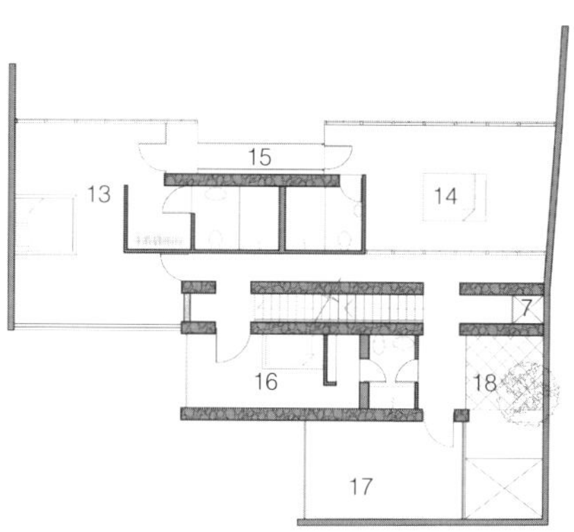

FIRST FLOOR PLAN

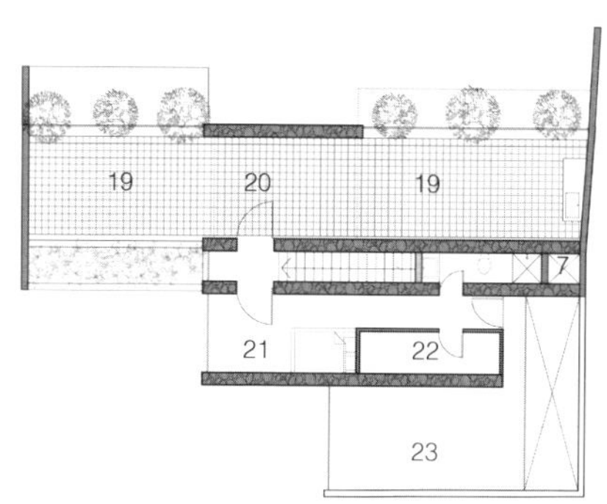

SECOND FLOOR PLAN

Kishan Perera House

Pelawatte

Architect **Vijitha Basnayaka**

The Kishan Perera House is a totally bespoke piece of architecture, that is to say it is designed specifically for the lifestyle of its owner, the proprietor of a car hire business. To carry out the work, the owner approached Vijitha Basnayaka who has a reputation of creating 'off the wall' designs. He first came to my notice with his 2000 design for the Mauli De Saram House that was constructed entirely of recycled building products and featured acrow props as structural roof supports.

Basnayaka studied at the Department of Architecture at the University of Moratuwa and

graduated in 1976. Now 60, he was in the third batch of students to graduate from the architecture school that was established at Moratuwa in 1972. His teachers were Ashley de Vos and Chris de Sarem. Later he returned to teach at Moratuwa and the work of some of his students also features in this book. He has now reduced his involvement in academia and concentrates on practice, mainly houses and currently a hotel in Habarana. He has also designed Rithihi, an exquisite sari shop in Alfred House Gardens in Colombo.

Basnayaka continues to promote building with recycled materials and in this, one of his most recent residential projects, he employs a wide palette of materials including corrugated metal sheets as interior wall cladding, hanging bamboo 'tats', exposed steel structural columns, brick and plaster. If the materials are less radical on this occasion, it is the ad hoc, idiosyncratic manner in which they are brought together that is intriguing and even disturbing to purists of architectural form.

Opposite: The living area looking towards the tall open-to-sky atrium above the koi pond.
Above: A view over the koi pond to the fluid space of the living and dining area. The first-floor circulation spaces overlook the central area.

The house is entered from the public street through a super wide pivoted door located centrally between two garage doors. Once inside, two diverging walls lead to an expansive open-to-sky atrium above a koi pond at the heart of the dwelling. The atrium is orientated approximately northwest to southeast and there are rooms on either side along with a 'bridge' connecting the master bedroom suite and three smaller bedrooms at first-floor level. One bedroom doubles as a home office.

The 'living room' is spatially akin to a hotel lobby and is indicated by a group of chairs around a low table rather than a physical enclosure. Beyond the atrium is a courtyard with a pale blue swimming pool. To the left is a guest bedroom suite with two wide sliding doors, so that the space is visually connected to the atrium. The service areas of the house are located to the right upon entering and an open riser stair leads to a first-floor balcony overlooking the atrium. The whole ground floor is a fluid space.

The interior of the house is truly an eclectic assemblage of disaggregated forms with inspiration apparently plucked from disparate sources. The kitchen has a brick arch that brings to mind an Italian pizza oven; the lightweight walls, sliding doors, joinery details and steps in front of the first-floor bedrooms have the appearance of a Japanese *ryokan*, and there is a bar in the living area with recycled ship portholes. In the dining area there is a raised 'stage'. Indeed, the whole interior has the appearance of a studio set for a TV sitcom or a stage set upon which various scenarios are enacted. This feeling is further promoted on a second visit by the sight of a high-powered motorcycle parked by the koi pond — effectively within the living room. The client's hobby is collecting antique cars and bikes and this space was designed to display them. In all, the house form and interior suggests a slightly unusual Bohemian lifestyle. The design can be read as a subversive act responding to conventional space planning.

Opposite: Beyond the living area is the formal dining area. Two recycled ship portholes are an intriguing feature of the bar area.
Above: A timber landing gives access to two bedrooms at first floor level. Curiously, the lightweight construction details elicit memories of a *ryokan*.
Left: The owner is a keen collector of vintage vehicles and a 1956 Triumph TR3 is displayed in the living room.

The large sliding doors at the southeast end of the living area and the tall atrium promote cross ventilation, while the bedrooms and the audiovisual room are air-conditioned. There are wide overhanging eaves and bamboo 'tats' mitigate heavy rain entering the living space. Iron bars above the open-to-sky roof are a typical local response to security requirements.

Basnayaka is keen to explain the process leading to the realisation of the house form and materials. He is sharply critical of trends in architecture towards design by computer that do not engage with craftsmen on site. "Design often stops at the office," he asserts. "More and more architects are disconnected from the site operatives; they do not understand materials and construction techniques. In some cases they do not speak the language of the craftsmen."

Because of these views, he is a proponent of lengthy discussion with craftsmen to resolve issues and details on site. The owner of the house, Kishan Perera, also became involved in these discussions so that the finished product is truly the result of a collaborative approach. "I am dedicated to the 'making' of architecture and to discussing details with the site artisans so that they participate in the design process," he states. He specifically includes in the design team D Siripala (responsible for masonry work), J P Saminda (responsible for carpentry work) and Raja (responsible for steel work), in addition to his assistants Ruminda Wijesuriya and Manuja Senevirathna.

"Houses should respond to climate and culture," asserts Basnayaka. By culture he doubtless refers to an evolving culture that is by definition a shifting target. The Kishan Perera house has the appearance of a hybrid dwelling that could change over time with additions and subtractions — there is a sense of impermanence. "Nothing lasts forever," says Basnayake in a reflective mood.

Opposite: Louvres and bamboo screens combine to give privacy and simultaneously allow air circulation.
Left: The kitchen and breakfast area have the ambience of an Italian pizza bar with an arch that employs exposed brickwork and plaster.

Above: The bedroom wing of the house with lightweight partition walls and under floor ventilation.

Above: The patio has a sparkling blue plunge pool shaded by palm trees. The architectural language adds to the eclectic sources employed by the architect.

Right: The internal environment is controlled by an array of bamboo screens, louvres and pergolas.

Opposite top and bottom: A wide pivoted door gives access to the house. The shifting geometry of the plan is arguably unique in the Sri Lankan context.

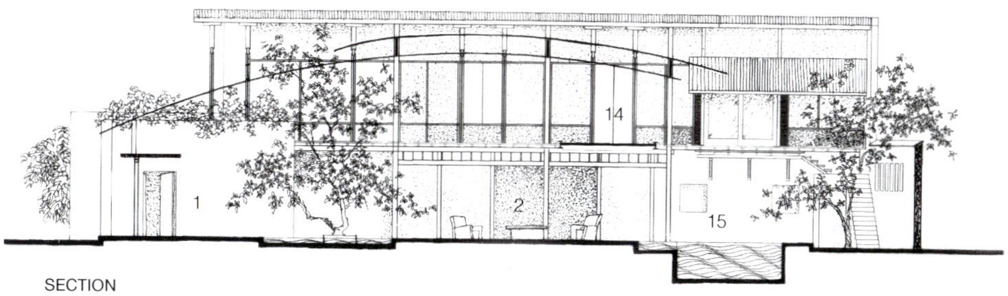

SECTION

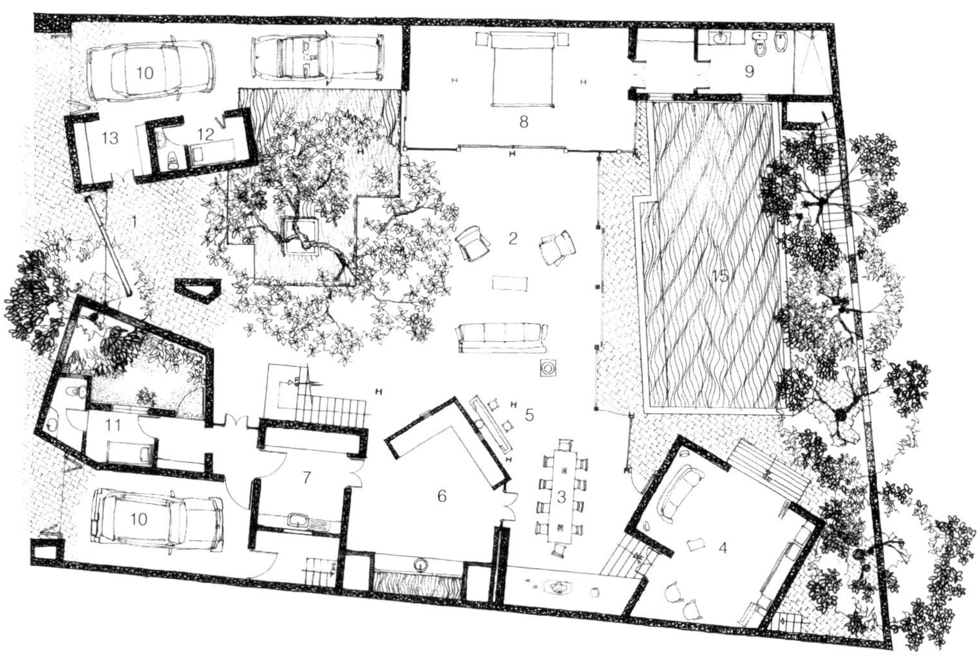

GROUND FLOOR PLAN

1	Entrance	9	Guest Bathroom
2	Living	10	Garage
3	Dining	11	Maid's Room
4	Audio / Visual	12	Driver's Room
5	Bar	13	Storage
6	Kitchen / Pantry	14	Bridge
7	Kitchen	15	Pool Court
8	Guest Bedroom		

Above: The house revolves around a tall open-to-sky courtyard with two tall trees. The ground floor living area is adjacent to the hard-paved space.
Right: The dining area is located on a mezzanine level overlooking the central courtyard.
Opposite: A window in the first floor study area also looks into the central space.

Abeyrathne House

Narahenpita, Colombo 05

Architect	Thisara Thanapathy *Thisara Thanapathy Architects*

The Abeyrathne House is an intriguing split-level urban house in the Narahenpita district in southeast Colombo. Completed in 2008, it is the home of a businessman, his wife and three children, one of whom is currently studying law in the UK. The street façade displays nothing of the internal arrangements and there are few exterior windows, but there is a total of five lightwells of varying sizes that bring daylight into the core of the house and facilitate natural ventilation. The largest of these is a dramatic open-to-sky hard-paved garden court at the heart of the dwelling to which all other spaces are related. Given the spatial constrains of a tight 250-square-metre urban site, the minimalist house is cleverly designed in section to permit a low-ceilinged garage to be inserted below a mezzanine floor. In this way four cars can be parked within the site without sacrificing valuable living space.

The architect is Thisara Thanapathy (50), who studied at the Department of Architecture at the University of Moratuwa from 1985 to 1992. Among others, he was taught by C Anjalendran in Year 1 (see pages 164–171 and 206–213) and by Vijitha Basnayaka (see page 190–197) in his later years. After graduation he worked for Ashley de Vos and Design Group 5 prior to setting up his own practice in 1999.

Thanapathy has great respect for the work of Geoffrey Bawa. "Bawa," he says, "had a spiritual link with the environment. There was a calming quality in his work." He also admires Kengo Kuma who blends tradition with modernity and Tadao Ando who, he thinks, adds a spiritual touch to all he creates. "In traditional cultures you have this spiritual quality," he explains. "I try to instill a sense of calmness and restraint in my own work. I try not to put my signature on the work. It involves a suppression of self."

The house is entered, somewhat unusually, at the junction of two urban streets. Six steps bring one, via a door, into a small entrance court with a tree and a bench where one may remove outdoor shoes. The courtyard acts as a buffer to reduce the noise and dust from the street. Turning sharply to the right from the entrance court one passes through a reception/living space

and beneath the master bedroom to arrive in the tall open-to-sky garden courtyard that is the focus of the house. Sunlight filters into the space through high-level louvres. Two trees climb to the source of light.

A square arched opening to the left leads to a third court with vertical circulation in the form of a staircase with a koi pond at the base. Ascending one half level gives access to the mezzanine dining area and kitchen. The dining area overlooks the garden court from a height of about 1.5 metres and beyond it is a service courtyard. The fifth court is at the lowest level alongside the entrance and lights a guest bedroom. The house is an intelligent response to the tropical climate: the use of courtyards together with the careful placement of windows and timber louvres ensures that there are comfortable conditions as well as visual privacy.

At the upper level, a master bedroom suite projects over the entrance and three smaller bedrooms all look into one or other of the internal courtyards through timber louvred shutters. The central garden court has a slightly austere feeling, but light floods into the space from above and the trees soften the space. A somewhat spartan steel and timber staircase with a steel balustrade ascends from the mezzanine to the higher levels. The finishes throughout are polished cement floors and unpainted cement walls in keeping with the minimalist aesthetic.

The house is an example of duality in residential planning in an urban situation where the outside expresses little of the lifestyle and status of the occupants while the inside is spacious, open and full of light. Perhaps it is not surprising in view of Sri Lanka's troubles in the past three decades that many houses turn inwards seemingly in a defensive gesture, away from public displays of wealth and towards a haven of peace. The architect believes the house "addresses deep human needs, such as peace of mind and relaxation. It rejects the pretentiousness of social images created by the consumerist culture."

"I have tried to create a tropical urban house with a modern Sri Lankan architecture which is neither a parody of the west nor a replication of Sri Lankan architecture from the past," Thanapathy concludes. The house was completed in 2008 and was the winner of the prestigious Geoffrey Bawa Award in 2011.

Opposite left and right: The main staircase ascends alongside a pond within a second open-to-sky lightwell. **Right:** A vertical view of the open-to sky space that lights and ventilates the stairwell.

SECTION

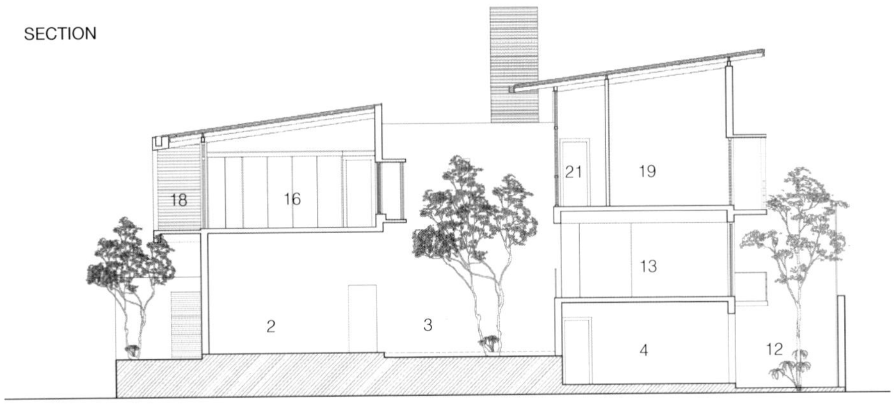

1 Entrance Court
2 Living
3 Courtyard
4 Garage
5 Garden
6 Guest Bedroom
7 Powder Room
8 Pond
9 Utility Room
10 Store Room
11 Servant's Room
12 Courtyard
13 Dining
14 Pantry
15 Kitchen
16 Master Bedroom
17 Master Bath / WC
18 Balcony
19 Bedroom
20 Bath / WC
21 Study

GROUND FLOOR PLAN

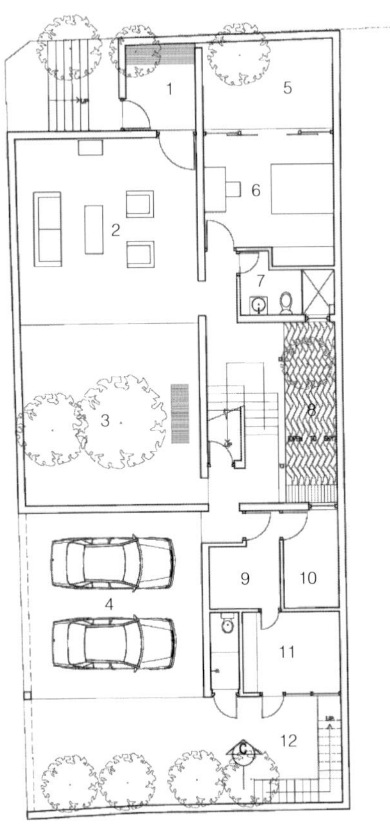

MEZZANINE FLOOR PLAN

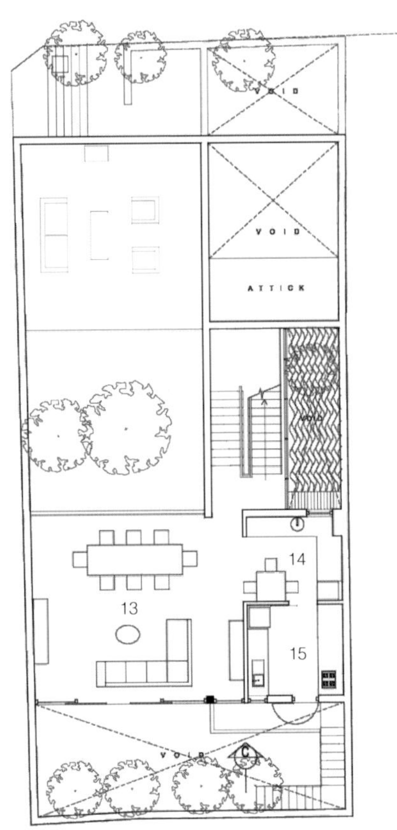

FIRST FLOOR PLAN

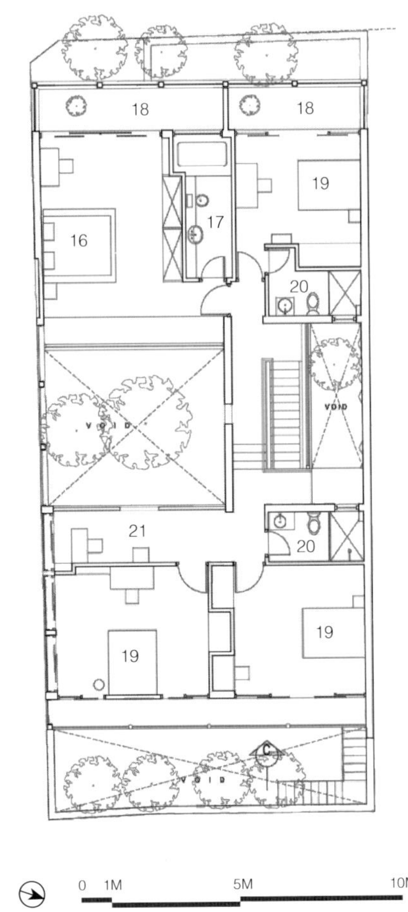

Above and far left: A high-ceilinged, naturally ventilated bedroom used by one of the owner's children.
Left: The children's study area with a window giving a view to the central courtyard.

Right: A 'love seat' in the living room is a replica of one used by Geoffrey Bawa in the Triton Hotel (1982). **Opposite:** The modest entrance to the house is enhanced by a hanging plumbago shrub and by the moonstone at the threshold.

Ranatunga House

Nawala

Architect C Anjalendran

The Ranatunga House, in a suburb of Colombo, is a skillfully designed urban dwelling where the architect, C Anjalendran, has distilled numerous ideas on a relatively small plot of land measuring 10 metres x 17 metres while simultaneously negotiating a considerable cross slope. The house is entered on a central axis, through a metal barred gate flanked on both sides by a garage space, but any notion of symmetry is immediately dispelled, for the transverse slope on the site requires that the garage to the left is four steps lower than the garage to the right. Alongside the entrance is small statue of a sitting Buddha. The vertical circulation core is also on the central axis with, to the left, a ground-floor office and to the right a guest/elderly relative's bedroom. To the rear of the staircase is a shared bathroom. There are oil lamps at the base of the stairs.

Ascending to the first floor, the central staircase gives access to the dining area and a double-height living area, both of which face out to the street over a planting trough that extends across the façade of the dwelling. Facing the rear of the house are a breakfast room, a kitchen, staff accommodation and a staff bathroom. Among the artifacts sourced by Anjalendran for the owners are a beautiful carved timber door from Jaffna, along with a 'love seat' and a painting by Channa Ekanayake. Anjalendran has also influenced the choice of colours used for decoration and some walls are painted a joyful cornflower yellow with columns in cobalt blue. Elsewhere blue diamond tiles are inlaid in polished cement floors.

Climbing to the second floor, the master bedroom/ study and the second bedroom look into the void above the living area. The former also enjoys views to the front and rear, while the balcony on the stairs also connects with the void. However, the outstanding feature of the house is experienced at third-floor level where

the staircase emerges at a splendid roof terrace with an open-sided pavilion and a fourth bedroom. The roof terrace has a planting trough above the street and also a diamond-shaped planter.

The house is designed to encourage stack ventilation, a system that works incredibly well. Air is drawn in through the ground-floor entrance grill and rises up the central stair, in the process ventilating all the rooms. Ceiling fans assist in the movement of air. The roof garden is exhilaratingly cool and is a place to escape from the stress of city life. Some time after the house was completed the owner acquired a parcel of land at the rear of the plot, so what was formerly a narrow rear courtyard is now an extensive green area with several mature trees.

The skilful manipulation of space, light and volumes is impressive and exhibits the principles that Anjalendran has passed on to an emerging generation of architects in his time as a teacher at both the Department of Architecture at the University of Moratuwa and the City School of Architecture in Colombo where he taught first-year students for nine years. "For me there are very basic rules," says Anjalendran, "all architecture should begin by being climatically sensitive and sustainable.

Above and opposite: The double-height living and dining room. The wood carving above the sofa is a recycled Sinhalese door. The painting to the left of the carved door is 'Abstract with Lotus' by Channa Ekanayake.

Opposite top: The rooftop pavilion looks out to the roof terrace. The columns have been, to quote the architect, 'painted blue for a new life'. **Opposite bottom left:** The stone statue on the trapezoidal garden is of a seated Vishnu, the Lord Protector. **Opposite bottom right:** Extensive planting at first floor level softens the street façade. **Above:** There is a panoramic view over the city from the roof terrace. **Overleaf left:** The artwork in the central staircase is a sun-based traditional motif designed by the Aluwihare Cooperative of Ena de Silva. **Overleaf right:** Another view of the staircase with a second artwork by Ena de Silva illustrating a Divisional Flag of Sri Lanka.

For example there should be cross ventilation and a stack effect (where the hot air rises and dissipates above). There should also be minimum glass, as this lets the heat in. In a tropical monsoon country you need a simple roof to keep away the sun and the rain, and you need air flowing through, to get rid of the humidity. In addition, build logically — place walls above walls to reduce costs."[1]

Anjalendran is critical of the spread of iconic architecture and architecture that has few ecological considerations. He espouses courtyards, verandahs and double skins that are generally missing from much contemporary architecture. Importantly, he believes sustainability in construction needs to be matched by sustainability in lifestyles. "There is a younger generation with a more technically advanced architecture," he notes, "However there is excess glass and an obsession with an alien aesthetic — a modernism derived from images from the West. I worry because these buildings are good to take photographs of, but they do not last climatically or socially."[2]

The exquisite Ranatunga House, though small, is ultimately a concise polemic statement of principles that Anjalendran has formulated to create affordable architecture that is appropriate for the climate of Sri Lanka. It is a modest low-energy and low budget house that achieves more with less.

[1] Anjalendran in conversation with Robert Powell, 9th February 2014.
[2] ibid.

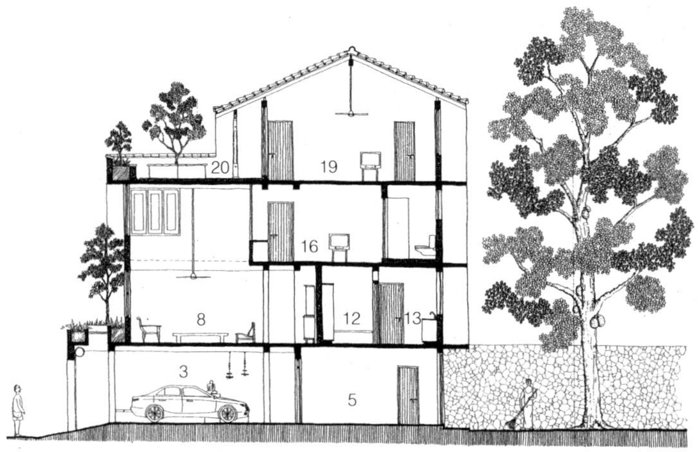

SECTION

1	Entrance	11	Kitchen
2	Reception	12	Maid
3	Garage	13	Maid's Bathroom
4	Office	14	Master Bedroom
5	Bedroom / Guest	15	Dressing Room / Computer
6	Bathroom / WC	16	Bedroom
7	Garden	17	Bathroom / WC
8	Living	18	Roof Pavilion
9	Dining	19	Bedroom
10	Breakfast / Pantry	20	Roof Terrace

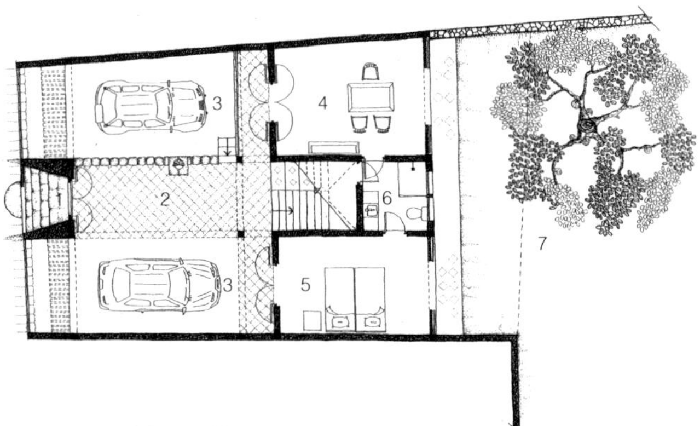

GROUND FLOOR PLAN

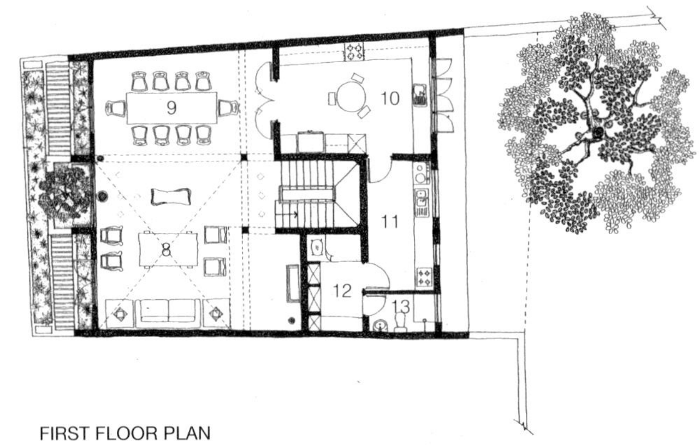

FIRST FLOOR PLAN

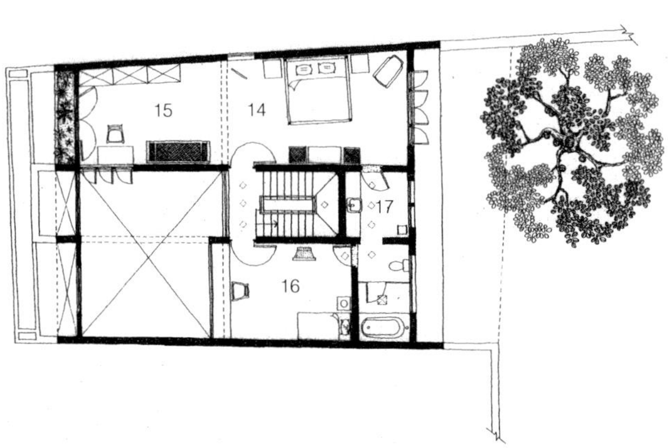

SECOND FLOOR PLAN

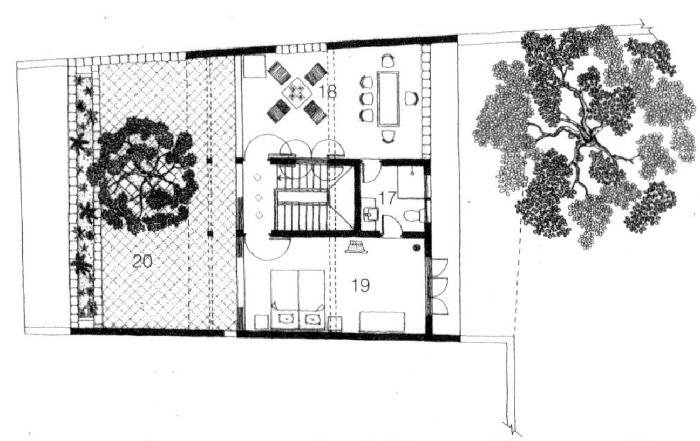

THIRD FLOOR PLAN

Siriwardena House

Mirihena

Architect	Philip Weera ratne and Don Thushar Jayamanne *PWA Architects*

The Siriwardena House in Mirihena is a sophisticated modern design for the owner of a trading company that deals mainly in bitumen products. He and his wife found their architect, Philip Weeraratne of PWA Architects, on the recommendation of a friend for whom he previously worked.

The house has an 'L'-shaped plan embracing a garden within a walled rectangular site. The plan is both simple and inventive. The dwelling is entered at the northern corner of the site, via a wonderful spatial sequence that leads through a double-height lobby and reception space spanned by a bridge and incorporating a pond with a waterfall, to a long gallery at right angles to the entrance. Salvaged columns from Jaffna are used non-structurally as decoration in the gallery that forms

one leg of the plan; this leads to the double-height living room and gives access to a ground-floor guest suite. From the living room and gallery there are views beyond a paved terrace and a plunge pool southeast to the garden. There are also views in the reverse direction into a linear landscaped courtyard that is parallel to the road. The accommodation is thus one-room-wide facilitating cross ventilation.

The second leg of the L-shaped plan extends directly from the entrance lobby to an open-sided dining area, passing in the process over a concrete bridge that spans the plunge pool, a powder room, a bar area with a discrete stair to the upper part of the house, and a pantry. Here, again, the principal rooms look into the garden. This wing of the house terminates at an open-to-sky barbecue area. The house gradually steps down the site that slopes from north to south, which adds another dimension.

The service areas are arranged in linear fashion along the northeast boundary and are separated from the main body of the house by a spine wall. They include a four-car garage, driver's accommodation, a generator, a kitchen, kitchen courtyard, utility room and staff accommodation.

At the upper level, the master bedroom has a direct link to the ground-floor living area via a library and looks into the garden. Two bedrooms for the owner's son also have garden views. Above the service area there is a gym, an audiovisual room and a Buddhist shrine room. There is also a roof terrace above the garage.

The designer of the house, Philip Weeraratne (44), studied architecture part-time at the City School of Architecture in Colombo from 1987 to 1995. He worked with Anura Ratnavibhushana for two years, then started his own practice in 1991 while still a student. His architectural language veers towards a well-crafted modernism with implicit references to the vernacular in the wide overhanging eaves, the low pitched roof, box gutters, multiple rainwater pipes integrated into columns, shading devices above ground-floor window openings, and polished cement floors. There is emphasis on natural ventilation and air-conditioning

is employed only in the bedrooms. It is an entrancing house at dawn when soft sunlight penetrates into the deepest part of the living room.

When the owners acquired the site, they essentially gave PWA a free hand. Philip Weeraratne refers to a "long process of distillation of the vernacular" to arrive at the modern architectural language employed in the design. It is a thoroughly organised plan with evidence that every detail has received rigorous attention. The house has the ambiance of a boutique resort with meticulous detailing. Yet if the strength and consistency of the architectural language threatens to overpower any expression of the owners' personality, it is balanced by their meticulous choice of antique chairs and tables, painted shutters from antiquity, and collector's artefacts such as an antique HMV gramophone. The house is ultimately a peaceful haven behind high walls.

Weeraratne firmly rejects nostalgia for the past and his admiration of the work of the Singapore-based architects Chan Soo Khian (with whom he has collaborated briefly) and Ernesto Bedmar, together with the experience of working alongside Tadao Ando and Shigeru Ban (see pages 108–115 and 100–107), indicates the criteria by which he wants his work to be judged.

Previous page: The elegant façades of the house face east and south towards the garden and are layered to mitigate the effects of solar heat gain. The canoe was acquired from an antique dealer in Borella, Colombo 8.
Opposite: A beautifully proportioned living room is at the heart of the house opening to a terrace overlooking the garden.
Above left: A bridge over the plunge pool connects the two wings of the L-shaped plan. To the right is a gallery leading to the living area.
Above right: A linear courtyard to the west of the living room assists in cross ventilation.

Above: The open-sided dining area connects directly to the garden. Sri Lankan architects and their clients have retained a relationship to the natural world that has almost disappeared in some tropical Asian countries.
Right: The plunge pool viewed from the living room terrace.
Far right: The library overlooking the living area.
Opposite: An open-riser staircase gives access to the roof from the drying yard for maintenance purposes.

1 Entrance Court
2 Lobby
3 Reception
4 Gallery
5 Living
6 Guest Bedroom
7 Guest Closet
8 Guest Bath / WC
9 Plunge Pool
10 Powder Room
11 Bar
12 Pantry
13 Dining
14 Barbeque
15 Garden
16 Kitchen
17 Kitchen Courtyard
18 Maid's Room
19 Toilet / Bath
20 Driver's Room
21 Generator
22 Garage
23 Master Bedroom
24 Closet
25 Master Bathroom
26 Library
27 Bridge
28 Bedroom
29 Bathroom / WC
30 Gym
31 Laundry Room
32 Shrine Room
33 TV Lounge
34 Roof Terrace
35 Drying Yard

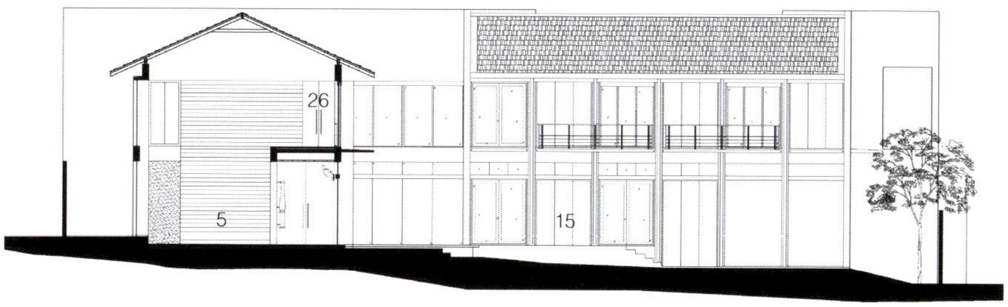

SECTION

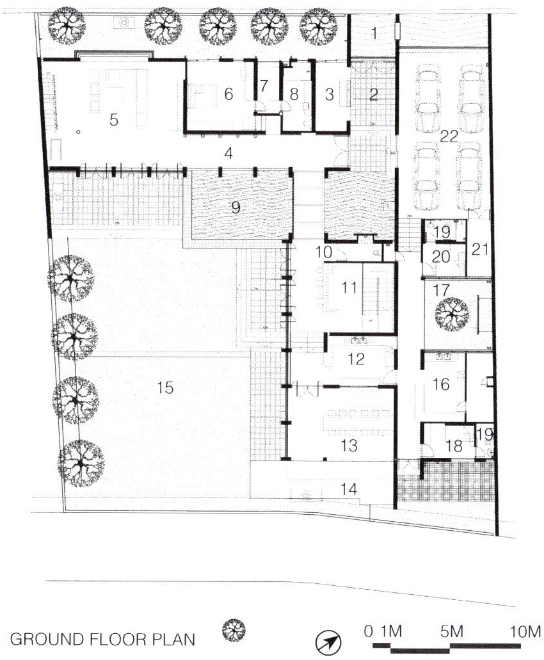

GROUND FLOOR PLAN

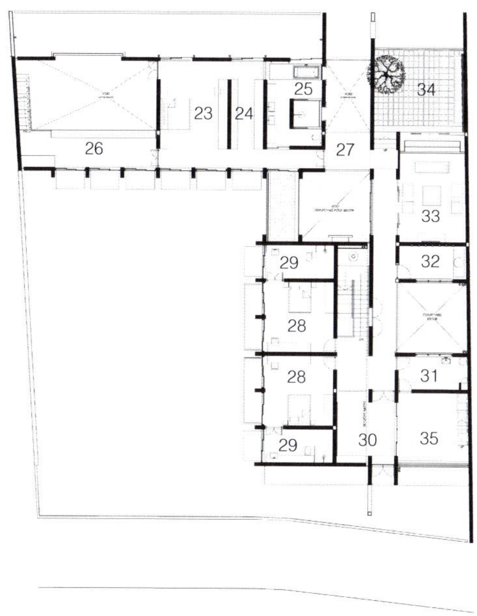

FIRST FLOOR PLAN

Bibliography

Bawa, Geoffrey, in *The Architecture of Housing* (Robert Powell Ed.), Exploring Architecture in Islamic Cultures, Aga Khan Trust for Culture, Geneva, 1990.

Champion, Stephen, *Sri Lanka War Stories*, Hotshop Books Ltd, Sri Lanka, 2008.

Correa, Charles, 'Transfers and Transformations' in *Charles Correa* (Hasan-Uddin Khan Ed.), Concept Media, Singapore, 1987.

De Chikera, Imara, 'Island Hideaway', *The Architect*, The Journal of the Sri Lanka Institute of Architects, Colombo, October 2012.

Fry, Maxwell and Jane Drew, *Tropical Architecture in the Dry and Humid Zones*, Batsford, London, 1964.

Inoon, Ayasha, 'A Modern Touch', *The Architect*, The Journal of the Sri Lanka Institute of Architects, Colombo, October 2009.

Jayawardene, Shanti, 'Bawa: A contribution to Cultural Regeneration' in *Mimar: Architecture in Development*, Aga Khan Award for Architecture, Concept Media, Singapore, No.19 January – March 1996.

Kadurugamuwa, Sonali, 'A Layered Duplex: Three Generations', *The Architect*, The Journal of the Sri Lanka Institute of Architects, April 2013.

Kannangara, Yashasvi, 'Designing a perfect balance between man and wilderness', *The Sunday Times*, Colombo, May 22nd 2011.

Khan, Hasan-Uddin and Charles Moore, 'The Architecture of the Individual House', in *The Architecture of Housing* (Robert Powell Ed.), Exploring Architecture in Islamic Cultures, The Aga Khan Award for Architecture, Geneva, 1990.

London, Geoffrey et al, *Kerry Hill: Crafting Modernism*, Thames and Hudson, London, 2013.

Pieris, Anoma, *Imagining Modernity: The Architecture of Valentine Gunasekara*, Pannipitiya, Stamford Lake (Pte) Ltd, Colombo, 2007.

Pieris, Anoma, *Architecture and Nationalism in Sri Lanka: The Trouser under the Cloth*, Routledge, 2012.

Plesner, Ulrik, *In Situ – An Architectural Memoir from Sri Lanka*, Narayana Press, Gyling, 2012.

Powell, Robert, 'Geoffrey Bawa – Seminal Works in Tropical Architecture' in the *Singapore Institute of Architects Journal*, July/August 1987.

Powell, Robert (Ed), *The Architecture of Housing*, Exploring Architecture in Islamic Cultures, The Aga Khan Award for Architecture, Geneva, 1990.

Powell, Robert, *The Asian House*, Select Books, Singapore, 1993.

Powell, Robert, *The Tropical Asian House*, Select Books, Singapore, 1996.

Powell, Robert, 'Beyond Bawa', *Singapore Institute of Architects Journal*, No 194/97, Singapore, 1997.

Powell, Robert, *The Urban Asian House*, Select Books, Singapore, 1998.

Powell, Robert, "Escape from the City: Armitage Hill" in *SPACE* 2000/04, Panpac Media, Singapore, August 2000.

Powell, Robert, 'A Courtyard Typology', in *SPACE* 2000/06, Panpac Media, Singapore, December 2000.

Powell, Robert, *The New Asian House*, Select Books, Singapore, 2001.

Prematilleke, Madhura, 'Beyond the Umbrella and other Stories," Annual Session of the Sri Lanka Institute of Architects, February 1997.

Richards, J M, 'Geoffrey Bawa', *Mimar: Architecture in Development*, Aga Khan Award for Architecture, Concept Media, Singapore, No.19 January – March 1996.

Robson, David, *Bawa: The Complete Works*, Thames and Hudson, London, 2002.

Robson, David, *Beyond Bawa*, Thames and Hudson, London, 2007.

Robson, David, *The Bawa Gardens*, Thames and Hudson, London, 2008.

Robson, David, *Anjalendran: An architect of Sri Lanka*, Tuttle, Singapore, 2009.

Shashidhar, Varna, 'Native Flavours', *www.betterinteriors* in April 2011.

Taylor, Brian Brace, *Geoffrey Bawa*, A Mimar Book, Concept Media, Singapore, 1986.

Architects' Directory

Kumudu Munasinghe
PAN ARCH (Pvt) Ltd
Architects and Engineers
Unit #1 Oceans 8
26/8 De Saram Road
Mount Lavinia
Sri Lanka
Tel: +94 (0) 112 719 793 / 452 7433
Mob: +94 (0) 714 712 304
Email: Kumuduarch@yahoo.com
www.panarch.lk

Channa Daswatte
MICD Associates
Chartered Architects
56/1, Pujya Sri Dharmaratne Mawatha
Madiwela
Kotte
Sri Lanka
Tel: +94 (0) 114 406 398
Mob: +94 (0) 777 343 449
Email: channadas@gmail.com
micd@eol.lk

C Anjalendran
60/8 Bogahena Road
Battaramulla
Sri Lanka
Tel: +94 (0) 112 872 197
Email: spotty@djls.net

Vinod Jayasinghe
Vinod Jayasinghe Associates (Pvt) Ltd
75 Pahalawela Road
Off Parliament Drive
Pelawatte
Battaramulla
Sri Lanka
Tel: +94 (0) 117 531 203
Mob: +94 (0) 777 305 871
Email: vjarchts@gmail.com

Palinda Kannangara
Chartered Architect
No. 405, Weliwala Road
Kotikawatta
Sri Lanka
Tel: +94 (0) 114 903 666/112419311
Mob: +94 (0) 777 326 830
Email: architectpalinda@yahoo.com
www.palindakannangara.com

Philip Weeraratne
and Ravindu Karunanayake
PWA Architects
5 Hamers Place
Colombo 6
Sri Lanka
Tel: +94 (0) 112 364 586
Mob: +94 (0) 777 352 856
Email: Philip@pwa.lk
Email: Info@pwa.lk
www.pwa.lk
or
Email: Phila@eureka.lk
projects@pwa.lk

Thisara Thanapathy
Thisara Thanapathy Architects
No 7/A Egodawatta Road
Boralesgamu
Sri Lanka
Tel: +94 (0) 112 545 901 / 011 2802716
Mob: +94 (0) 77 982 2426
Email: thisarat@sltnet.lk
Email: thisarathanapathy@gmail.com
www.thanapathyarchitects.com

Waruna Gomis
I W Associates (Pvt) Ltd
309/3, Pelawatta Road
Bollegala 11630
Gonawala (Western Province)
Sri Lanka
Tel: +94 (0) 11 306 5266
Mob: +94 (0) 777 446 391
Email: waruna.gms@gmail.com

Sudesh Nanayakkara
Chartered Architect
404, Nawala Road
Rajagiriya
Sri Lanka
Tel : +94 (0) 773 792 678
Email: sudeshnanayakkara10@gmail.com

Godridge Samuel
MMGS Architects
26A Alwis Place
Colombo 3
Sri Lanka
Tel: +94 (0) 11 2439294
Mob: +94 (0) 777 766 511
Email: mmgs@sltnet.lk
www.mmgsarchitects.com

Pradeep Kodikara
Guildford Crescent
Colombo 7
Sri Lanka
Tel: +94 (0) 777 144 379
Email: pkodikara@gmail.com

Ragi Kadirgamar
261/18 Poorvarama Road
Kirilapone
Colombo 5
Sri Lanka
Tel: +94 (0) 777 366 034
+91 (0) 770 834 7908
Email: Ragi_infinity@yahoo.com

Shayan Kumaradas
55, Pamankada Lane
Colombo 6
Sri Lanka
Tel: +94 (0) 777 667 616
Email: shayankumaradas@gmail.com
shayan.skca@gmail.com

Tadao Ando
Tadao Ando Architect & Associates
www.tadao-ando.com

Shigeru Ban
Shigeru Ban Architects Europe
6, Rue de Braque, 75003,
Paris
France
Tel : +33 (0)1 70 71 20 50
Email: europe@shigerubanarchitects.com

Architects' Directory, ctd

Kerry Hill
Kerry Hill Architects
29 Cantonment Road
Singapore 089746
Tel: +65 6323 5400
Email: kerry@kerryhillarchitects.com
www.kerryhillarchitects.com

Ranjan Aluwihare
RA Designs
6, Gomes Path (Off De Fonseka Rd)
Colombo 05
Sri Lanka
Tel: +94 (0)777 584 630
+94 (0) 112 586708
rickshaw@applesri.com
www.ra-designs.lk

Madhura Prematilleke
Team ARCHITRAVE
55, 5th Lane
Colombo 03
Sri Lanka
Tel: +94 (0) 11 471 7196
Mob: +94 (0) 777 346 299
Email: madhuradirect@gmail.com
www.teamarchitrave.com

Sanath Liyanage
S L A Architects Pvt Ltd
766/3, Samagi Mawatha
Erawwala
Pannipitiya
Sri Lanka
Tel : +94 (0) 11 7202921,
Mob: +94 (0) 777 487 761
Email: liyanagesanath@gmail.com
slaarchitectspvtltd@gmail.com

Vijitha Basnayaka
N V W Basnayaka
'Rohini', Bolatha
Ganemulla
Sri Lanka
Tel: +94 (0) 772 368 131
vbasnayaka@gmail.com

Amila de Mel
Chartered Architect
No 53 Ward Place
Colombo 07
Sri Lanka
Tel: +94 (0) 11 269 3634
Mob: +94 (0) 777 373 230
amilademel@gmail.com

Author
Robert Powell
R5 Marine Gate
Marine Drive
Brighton
BN2 5TN
UK
Tel: +44 (0) 1273 624855
Email: robert_powell42@yahoo.co.uk
www.robertpowell-architect.com

Photographer
Sebastian Posingis
www.sebastianposingis.com

Introductory Essays
David Robson
Flat 21
Furze Croft
Furze Hill
Hove BN3 1PB
UK
Tel: +44 (0) 1273 202381
greensett@gmail.com

Publisher
Ian Pringle
Talisman Publishing Pte Ltd
52 Genting Lane
06–05
Ruby Land Complex 1
Singapore 349560
Tel: +65 6749 3551
Fax: +65 6749 3552
Email: ian@apdsing.com
www.apdsing.com

Acknowledgements

In compiling this book on new residential architecture in Sri Lanka I have been assisted by numerous individuals.

The book was made possible by a fruitful collaboration with David Robson who sourced many of the houses and made introductions to architects and house owners. He unselfishly opened many doors to me. I thank him for his excellent introductory essays setting the current work in context.

Secondly I have to express my appreciation of photographer Sebastian Posingis. It is the first time we have worked together and Sebastian shouldered the logistics of travelling in Sri Lanka at the same time showing a wonderful ability to take everything in his stride and produce outstanding pictures. Both Sebastian and I are also indebted to Manih Ahmed for his generous contribution towards the book's production.

Thirdly I have to record my debt to the following owners of houses for their generosity in opening their homes and revealing their lifestyles:
Kumudu and Amithayapa Munasinghe, Channa Daswatte, Ajith and Chandani Gunawardana, Ashan and Swasha Malalsekera, Lakshan and Samurdi Hettiarachchi, Prabodha Sumanasekera, Firaz, Varuna and Shehani Maliduwapathirana, Fiona Mendis, Krishan and Menaka Balendra, Godridge and Beulah Samuel, L Samson Amal and Himarsha De Silva, Vikrom Mathur, Koenraad Pringier, Pierre and Saskia Pringiers, Kerry and Ruth Hill, Nadeem Qureshi, S. K. Sivakumaren and Vasuki Sivakumaren, Mark Green, Nirmal and Olivia Madanayake, Sanjeewa Maddumage, Ranjan and Shaunagh Aluwihare, Kishan Perera, Sarath and Rohini Abeyrathne, Ashoka and Nadira Siriwardena, Chaminda and Apsara Ranatunga, Amila de Mel and Sarath Samarasinghe.

My special thanks go to Miles Young who provided a base in Colombo and Mirissa.

Fourthly I have to thank the following architects and interior designers for their enthusiasm and willingness to explore new directions in the architecture of Sri Lanka:
Channa Daswatte, Kumudu Munasinghe, Palinda Kannangara, Vinod Jayasinghe, Waruna Gomis, Sudesh Nanayakkara, Godridge Samuel, Pradeep Kodikara, Shigeru Ban, Philip Weeraratne, Ravindu Karunanayake, Tadao Ando, Kerry Hill, Madhura Prematilleke, Shayan Kumaradas, Ragi Kadirgamar, Sanath Liyanage, Thisara Thanapathy, Ranjan Aluwihare, Vijitha Basnayake and Amila de Mel.

I wish in particular to thank C Anjalendran for sourcing houses for inclusion and for his encouragement, support and generosity while we were researching the book.

I have to acknowledge my Singapore Director Lynda Lim Kwee Guek for her continuing support over three decades and other individuals including Priyanka Magdum, Hirante Welandawe, Varuna de Silva, Narein Perera, Akila Nikapitiya, Ajith Fernando, Kumar, Dominic and Nazreen Sansoni, Kasun Jayamanne, Justin Hill, Simon Cundy, R H Amila Gayan De Silva, Jennifer Henricus, Suranga Tennakoon, Nadun Suputhantri, Chisato Kodaira, Shiromal Cooray, Milinda and Evangeline Ekanayake, Chamika De Alwis and K Shanika who assisted in a myriad ways.

I thank our publisher Ian Pringle for his belief in the book and the staff at Talisman Publishing — Janice Ng, Stephy Chee, Foo Chee Ying and Norreha Sayuti for their commitment to a high quality publication. I am grateful to Kim Inglis for her meticulous text editing and I am indebted to Madhura Prematilleke for his incisive comments on my introductory essay.

Finally I thank my wife Shantheni Chornalingam Powell and our daughter Zara Shakira for their love and unwavering support.

First published in 2015
This paperback edition 2026

Talisman Publishing Pte Ltd
talisman@apdsing.com
www.talismanpublishing.com
ISBN 978-981-94-5734-2

Editor Kim Inglis

Art Director Norreha Sayuti

Designer Stephy Chee, Foo Chee Ying

Studio Manager Janice Ng

Publisher Ian Pringle

Printed in Malaysia